Working Together in the
Body of Christ

Working Together in the Body of Christ

1 Corinthians

This inductive Bible study is designed for individual, small group, or classroom use. A leader's guide with full lesson plans and the answers to the Bible study questions is available from Regular Baptist Press. Order RBP0096 online at www.regularbaptistpress.org, e-mail orders@rbpstore.org, call toll-free 1-800-727-4440, or contact your distributor.

Regular Baptist Press
Building Lives by the Book
www.RegularBaptistPress.org

The Doctrinal Basis of Our Curriculum

A more detailed statement with references is available upon request.

- The verbal, plenary inspiration of the Scriptures
- Only one true God
- The Trinity of the Godhead
- The Holy Spirit and His ministry
- The personality of Satan
- The Genesis account of creation
- Original sin and the fall of man
- The virgin birth of Christ
- Salvation through faith in the shed blood of Christ
- The bodily resurrection and priesthood of Christ
- Grace and the new birth
- Justification by faith
- Sanctification of the believer
- The security of the believer
- The church
- The ordinances of the local church: baptism by immersion and the Lord's Supper
- Biblical separation— ecclesiastical and personal
- Obedience to civil government
- The place of Israel
- The pretribulation rapture of the church
- The premillennial return of Christ
- The millennial reign of Christ
- Eternal glory in Heaven for the righteous
- Eternal torment in Hell for the wicked

Alex Bauman, editor
WORKING TOGETHER IN THE BODY OF CHRIST: 1 CORINTHIANS
Adult Bible Study Book
Vol. 62, No. 2
© 2013
Regular Baptist Press • Schaumburg, Illinois
www.regularbaptistpress.org • 1-800-727-4440
Printed in U.S.A.
All rights reserved
RBP0099 • ISBN: 978-1-60776-826-5

Contents

Preface 7

Lesson 1 A Plea for Unity 9

Lesson 2 God's Reliable Word 17

Lesson 3 The Church's One Foundation 25

Lesson 4 Just Be Faithful!. 35

Lesson 5 It's a Tough Job, but 43

Lesson 6 Family Matters 51

Lesson 7 Marriage: Knotted or Not? 59

Lesson 8 Give Me Liberty and Love 67

Lesson 9 The Church at Worship 77

Lesson 10 You Are Gifted 87

Lesson 11 Tongues Talk 97

Lesson 12 Up from the Grave 105

Lesson 13 A Heart for Giving 115

Preface

Christ is the head of the church while believers form His body. He gives us all direction and empowers us by the Spirit, but we must work together like a well-oiled machine in our local churches if we hope to accomplish His will. One frozen gear or broken pin will keep a church from working effectively.

The first century body of believers at Corinth was in bad shape. That church had gears refusing to budge while others were moving in the wrong direction. And many of the parts had snapped rendering them totally ineffective. The church was broken. Paul wrote the Corinthians believers an instruction manual and challenged them to start working together to accomplish God's will.

You have the privilege of reading Paul's instruction manual and considering how it applies to your own body of believers. You will find that the problems in Corinth are not too different than the problems churches face today. And the solutions are timeless.

Allow 1 Corinthians to challenge you personally. Consider your part in your local body of Christ. Have you seized? Are you moving in the wrong direction? Are you broken and in need of repair?

A Plea for Unity

Believers need to be team players in their local church, grateful for their salvation, and dedicated to the goal of glorifying God.

1 Corinthians 1

"Now I beseech you, brethren, by the name of our Lord Jesus Christ, that ye all speak the same thing, and that there be no divisions among you; but that ye be perfectly joined together in the same mind and in the same judgment" (1 Corinthians 1:10).

Someone once said, "We could learn a lot from crayons; some are sharp, some are pretty, some are dull, while others bright, some have weird names, but they all have learned to live together in the same box."

While a church is not a crayon box, it certainly has diverse team members. How those members work together will go a long way in determining the true success of the church. The Corinthian church needed instruction on functioning as a team. Paul encouraged their loyalty to Christ.

Getting Started

1. What are the characteristics of a team whose members successfully play or work together?

2. Describe a team whose members do not work well together.

3. What part do you think teamwork plays in a church's success?

Searching the Scriptures

Often, we think churches in the first century were immune to the problems we see in some churches today. As we study 1 Corinthians, however, we discover that the church at Corinth was riddled with serious problems. These included disunity, feuding, spiritual pride, carnality, covetousness, and immorality. The Corinthians needed to turn their attention to Christ, the head of the Church, and give Him their love and loyalty. Cooperating with one another under the headship of Christ, they would fulfill God's purpose for them and be shining lights in a spiritually dark city. Our witness, too, will be much stronger if we apply the principles we find in 1 Corinthians.

Some believers wanted personal acclaim and formed their own little groups within the congregation. They put personal interests ahead of God's glory and coveted one another's spiritual gifts. Instead of helping to build up the church, they behaved in a manner that threatened to destroy it.

Corinth's Background

Investigating the location and cultural background of this city helps us understand the context of the instruction that Paul provides them.

An economic center of its region, Corinth had a population of approximately 600,000. Corinth was a strategically located, well-traveled commercial center. The city was modern for its time with paved streets, gutters, and pedestrian walkways. They had even developed an elaborate system that allowed ships to traverse the isthmus where Corinth was located, thus avoiding the treacherous journey around the south end of the Peloponnesian Peninsula. This attracted many travelers and contributed greatly to Corinth's cosmopolitan culture.

Corinth also benefited from fertile fields and a good supply of spring water, but along with the prosperity came taverns and night clubs.

The pagan Temple of Aphrodite, with its 1,000 priestesses, dominated the religious scene in Corinth. It contributed to rampant prostitution and immorality. Eventually the term "corinthianize" came to represent gross immorality and drunkenness. The city was also known for crime.

4. How does Corinth compare to your city in terms of population, economy, health, and spiritual climate?

5. What might you include in a composite character sketch of a typical Corinthian? (See 1 Cor. 6:9–11; 11:18–22.)

6. What kind of witness might have been required to reach the typical Corinthian for Christ?

Saved by God's Grace

Paul opens his first inspired letter to the Corinthians by appealing for unity. He reminded them that all were saved by God's grace for His glory.

Outwardly, Christians have different backgrounds and tastes. But these distinctions are not of ultimate importance. All Christians are members of God's family.

In a local church, Christians are members of the same family and the same team. They are coworkers with God, striving to advance the gospel and glorify the Lord within their communities. Christians are saved by grace alone, and grace enables them to be productive team players.

Paul attributed his salvation and his Christian service to the grace of God (Eph. 2:8, 9; 1 Cor. 15:10). God saved him by grace and by grace God enabled him to serve as an apostle.

In presenting his apostolic credentials to the Corinthian church (1 Cor. 1:1), Paul was citing his authority for writing to reprove their sins, challenge their practices, and direct their behavior. He was not alone in his stance. Sosthenes, apparently the man mentioned in Acts 18:17 as the former "chief ruler of the synagogue" in Corinth, was with Paul when he wrote this letter. He, too, owed everything to the grace of God, for he was a "brother" in the family of God (1 Cor. 1:1).

The Corinthian Christians had not done anything to gain their favored standing in God's sight. God had set them apart from pagan society and had summoned them to be His holy people (1:2). Like Paul and Sosthenes, the Christians at Corinth owed everything to the grace of God.

7. Read 1 Corinthians 1:1–9. What had God done for the Corinthian Christians?

8. What has God's grace accomplished in your life?

The Corinthian Christians needed a constant supply of the grace of God as well as the peace of God. Paul prayed for the supply of both to come from the Father through Jesus Christ (1:3). Without these provisions, the church would be a frustrated failure.

God's Activity in Believers

Paul was grateful for the divine grace God showed his readers (1:4).

By investing spiritual gifts in the Corinthian Christians, God proved He had saved them. The Corinthian church was blessed with gifted communicators of the gospel (1:5, 6). God had equipped the Corinthians with spiritual gifts to serve Him effectively until the Rapture, if it were to occur in their lifetime (1:7). By His grace, the Corinthian Christians would stand blameless in Christ's presence in that day (1:8). They could trust God's faithfulness—not their own—to accomplish such a feat (1:9).

The Corinthians should have recognized what they had in common: They owed everything they were and had to the grace of God. By grace they were members of God's family, equipped to serve Him. This should have persuaded them to worship and work unitedly.

9. Respond to the following statement: God's grace is the great equalizer among believers in the church.

Saved for God's Glory

God created man to glorify Him, but Adam plunged the human race into sin. Since that dark day, the human race has dishonored God. However, saved members of the race can glorify God because God's Spirit is patiently conforming them to the image of Christ (cf. Rom. 8:29).

Although the Corinthians were saints (1:2), they did not glorify God (cf. 10:31). They had a misplaced trust in human leadership. Instead of having unity of purpose, they formed cliques, or "divisions" based on "contentions" (1:10, 11). Some boasted that they were Paul's disciples. Others claimed to follow Apollos or Cephas. Still others claimed to belong only to Christ (1:12). Such divisions fragmented the church and spoiled its testimony, hindering the work and detracting from the glory of God.

10. What problems might the presence of cliques cause in a church?

To combat this error, Paul confronted his readers with the fact that Jesus Christ deserves singular devotion. Human leaders must neither be objects of worship nor lords over others. Only Christ died on the cross in our place. Believers are baptized in Christ's name and not in the name of an apostle (1:13). Apparently, some Christians at Corinth claimed to have been baptized in Paul's name or in the name of Apollos or Cephas. They built their lives around their baptizer. Paul disclaimed his importance as a baptizer and emphasized the importance of Calvary (1:14–17).

11. What is the difference between commendable loyalty to a spiritual leader (1 Cor. 11:1) and inappropriate loyalty?

12. What evidence of inappropriate devotion to religious leaders do you observe today?

13. What might motivate a religious leader to draw a following?

14. How could a discipler or a pastor motivate others to be loyal followers of Christ?

No Reason to Exude Pride

Drawing the Corinthians' attention to Christ, Paul focused on God's wisdom in saving sinners on the basis of Christ's sacrifice at Calvary (1 Cor. 1:18). The worldly wise scoff at the preaching of the Cross, but God's Word about the Cross leads sinners to salvation through faith in Christ (1:19–21).

Pride rejects the work of the Cross; faith appropriates it. The Corinthian church members needed to proclaim the Cross, not following men.

No one can rightfully boast about his merits if he understands the significance of Christ's death on the cross. Christ died for helpless, hopeless sinners. He did for us what we could not do for ourselves.

The crucifixion announces that we deserved nothing from God except eternal condemnation. It proclaims inexplicable love, mercy, and grace. It serves notice that God accepts us in spite of our record, not because of it. No one can reason his way to God.

The Corinthian Christians should have been motivated by the Cross to exercise great humility and begin working as a team. But neither Jews nor Gentiles are prone to believe in the Christ of Calvary. Paul makes very specific arguments about the reasons why in each case.

The Jews said they required supernatural demonstrations before they would believe in Christ (1:22a; cf. John 2:18; 4:48). Yet they refused to repent when they saw Him perform miracles that confirmed that He was the Jewish Messiah (John 20:30, 31). The miracles both displayed Christ's divine power and showed His qualifications to be king in the coming Millennial Kingdom (Isa. 35:5, 6; cf. Matt. 11:4–6).

The Greeks rejected the proclamation of the Cross because it did not make any sense to them (1:22b). Some of the Greeks believed matter, including man, was evil while gods were spiritual and good. In their estimation, a god would not and could not become a man. And a god certainly would never die on a cross to secure the salvation of people. They believed gods were completely uninterested in humanity. In such a society, the message of the cross was just plain foolish.

Furthermore, Greek philosophers were not interested in a relationship with God. They thrived on debates, questions, and human wisdom.

Teaching about the Cross was a stumbling block to the Jews and foolishness to the Gentiles (1:23). So was the gospel insufficient for the Jews and Greeks? Did the gospel need help? Would yet another sign help the Jews or more evidence help the Greeks? No. The gospel was powerful in Paul's day, and it still is today. As we share it, God's grace works in the hearts and minds of some of those who hear it to help them see their need for salvation and respond accordingly. By grace God called individual Jews and Gentiles to salvation (1:24; cf. 2 Thess. 2:13, 14).

What so many perceived as foolishness and weakness on God's part was actually far greater than human wisdom and power (1:25).

15. Read 1 Corinthians 1:25. How does it encourage you to know that the foolishness and weakness of God, if He could be those, would be wiser and stronger than men?

Although the Jews and Gentiles as a whole rejected the preaching of the Cross, God saved some from both groups, including even some of this world's "wise men" (1:16). In fact, the Christians at Corinth had been saved from both Jewish and Gentile backgrounds (1 Cor. 12:2). Few of them had been prominent members of society, but by grace all of them had become

God's people (1 Cor. 1:26–28). Since they could not boast about themselves, they could only rightfully boast about God's grace (1:29, 31).

God had united them to His Son, and in Christ they had wisdom, righteousness, a holy separation unto God, and redemption. They were free from slavery to sin and free to serve the Lord (1:30).

Their only message was the eternal truth of God's Word. Acting in obedience, they could impact Corinth mightily with the gospel. It is more powerful than any sign and more profound than any human wisdom.

Paul summoned the Corinthians to unity. Instead of following personalities, these Christians were supposed to follow the Lord in humility. It was incumbent upon the Christians to present a clear witness about the saving power of the Cross to the glory of God to wicked Corinth.

Today's society, too, needs the gospel. Let us present it to them and then support our words with attractive living. Let us glorify God, being what we ought to be and doing what we ought to do.

Making It Personal

16. Consider how loyalties to self might interfere with teamwork in the church. What personal loyalties could make your church dysfunctional?

17. What dysfunctional loyalties might you have?

18. Why do believers in a local church need to function as a team?

19. What could you do to help build a united team in your church?

20. Memorize 1 Corinthians 1:10.

God's Reliable Word

The Bible, God's fully inspired and reliable Word, forms the basis of our ministry and message.

1 Corinthians 2

"And my speech and my preaching was not with enticing words of man's wisdom, but in demonstration of the Spirit and of power: That your faith should not stand in the wisdom of men, but in the power of God" (1 Corinthians 2:4, 5).

Rome may have had the first mail service. The city started delivering mail not too many years before Paul during the reign of Augustus Caesar. The "mail trucks" were carriages pulled by horses. Government used the service at first with service for citizens added later. The messages crisscrossing the Roman Empire were important.

That is not like today. Over half the mail delivered today is junk mail—not exactly important and personal messages. That must make delivering mail in the middle of a blizzard an even more unpleasant job.

Paul was not a mail carrier, but he gladly braved all kinds of adversity to deliver a message to as many people as possible. That personal message came from God and was addressed to "whosoever will" (Rev. 22:17).

Getting Started

1. If you were as effective at delivering the mail as you are at witnessing, would you still have a job as a mail carrier?

2. What might someone conclude about the importance of the gospel based on your life?

Searching the Scriptures

God's Word Proclaimed

Paul did not use worldly methods of persuasion in presenting the gospel. Recalling his first visit to Corinth, he assured his readers he had not delivered masterfully constructed speeches simply to show off his wisdom and oratorical skills (1 Cor. 2:1). His message was simple but powerful; he preached "Jesus Christ, and him crucified" (2:2). Paul's confidence was not in his ability as a speaker but in the ability of the Holy Spirit to use the clear and simple message of the Cross to persuade the Corinthians to trust in the Savior (2:3–5).

Paul viewed himself as a herald, delivering a message of crucial importance and extreme urgency from the Majesty on high. His responsibility, as he saw it, was to deliver the message in such a way that the audience would understand it and heed it. He did not obscure the message by trying to embellish it. Nor did he detract from it by drawing attention to himself. He was not there to amuse the Corinthians with his oratory as they were accustomed to in the secular Greek culture.

3. Is it wrong to desire that your pastor preach in an engaging manner? Explain.

4. Is it wrong for the preacher to focus on engaging his audience? Explain.

While there certainly is a danger in focusing too heavily on the use of oratory or eloquence in preaching and teaching, this does not seem to be Paul's ultimate emphasis in 1 Corinthians 2:1–5. Rather, Paul's emphasis is that he proclaimed Christ and the Cross, not some carefully drafted message that appealed to human ingenuity and cleverness. He was teaching the wisdom of God, not the wisdom of man.

Paul's message was not an easy one to deliver. First, the gospel is not an easy message. Furthermore, Paul's words in this inspired epistle challenged the Corinthians' understanding and their will to obey. Thus, Paul determined from the beginning not to make his teaching more complicated than necessary. As often as possible, he appealed to the Corinthians using "the simplicity that is in Christ" (2 Cor. 11:3).

5. Read 1 Corinthians 2:2–4. What was Paul's initial purpose in coming to Corinth?

6. How was this evident in his ministry?

Paul's initial purpose in coming to Corinth resulted in an epistle that draws sharp contrasts between the wisdom of God and the thinking of a church that was formerly steeped in the worldly thinking of Greek philosophy. The epistle, then, is a manual for dealing not only with church problems, but also with secular philosophies and the evil fruit they bear.

Paul indicated he was weak and fearful when he visited Corinth (1 Cor. 2:3). He meant that he trembled at the seriousness of his responsibility and at the seriousness of the message he conveyed. He feared the Corinthians, who desperately needed the gospel, would reject the message of salvation.

7. What do you remember about Corinth from lesson 1 that might have given Paul reason to fear the Corinthians would reject the gospel?

No doubt Paul also feared he might rely on his own inadequate ability to deliver the message. This is a battle we all face as believers. We are tempted to use cleverness, manipulation, or emotional appeals in presenting the gospel. But those methods often lead to insincere decisions.

8. Read 1 Corinthians 2:4, 5. Why is it important to share the gospel with a reliance on the Holy Spirit's power?

Notice that it was the inward "demonstration of the Spirit" (2:4) that Paul considered more powerful than any sign miracle or any word of eloquent wisdom. The same "power" that Paul had is available to us today through the Holy Spirit whenever we teach God's self-authenticating Word. He will use it to call some to the gospel (cf. 1:24).

9. Do you think it is possible to sweep away all objections to the Bible by debating intelligently in the Bible's defense? Why or why not?

The very fact that Paul was plain-speaking, weak, and fearful made it clear that the Corinthian converts were drawn to Christ by the Spirit and not by the wisdom and charm of the speaker. Clearly, Paul revered God's Word. He did not try to embellish it; he just preached it as it was to people as they were.

As in Paul's day, so now much more in these closing days of the church age, the tendency is to minimize the Cross and the Gospel and streamline the message to present something that is more palatable and seemingly relevant to the listener and the culture. Thus, like Paul, our only reasonable course is to proclaim "Jesus Christ, and him crucified" (1 Cor. 2:2).

Moreover, we can gain confidence that if Paul's simple gospel could win the day at Corinth, its power can triumph anywhere. Paul ministered to the Corinthians because of their overwhelming spiritual needs, not because it was a natural setting to build a thriving ministry. The gospel is not a commodity to be dispensed only where it will produce the greatest yield by human standards.

10. What does Paul's ministry at Corinth say about the gospel's power?

God's Word Portrayed

Paul was not opposed to wisdom. He is certainly not saying that ministers should not give themselves to gaining true, Biblical wisdom and to understanding theological precision. Although he did not adopt and use worldly wisdom, which God will destroy (1:19), he did "speak wisdom" (2:6). This wisdom was well received among those who appreciated the message of the Cross (2:6). They perceived the Cross to be the greatest manifestation of God's wisdom (2:7, 8).

The whole Bible points to Calvary as the place where God provided redemption in Christ. Even before He launched the ages of human history, God in wisdom planned the Cross (cf. Acts 2:23; 1 Pet. 1:19, 20; Rev.13:8). God's wisdom presents His Son's death on the cross as the solution to the sin problem, but this wisdom is hidden to unbelievers (1 Cor. 2:7).

11. Read 1 Corinthians 2:8. What do Paul's words say about "the princes of this world"?

In the death of God's Son man proved his spiritual ignorance, but God proved His infinite wisdom.

12. Share how your view about Christ's death changed dramatically when the Holy Spirit enlightened your mind to the truth of the gospel.

13. Share a personal discovery of an encouraging truth in the Bible.

God's Word Revealed—Revelation

Three important terms apply to the communication of God's Word to us and to our understanding of it. The first of these terms is "revelation."

The term "revelation" may be defined as a disclosure of truth from God, which would be unknowable without that disclosure. Human wisdom cannot comprehend spiritual truth. The scientific method cannot uncover it. Higher education cannot fathom it. Human senses cannot grasp it (2:9).

However, God has given us His Word, which supplies all we need to know about His plans and provisions for us (2:10). The Holy Spirit imparted this wonderful revelation from God to us (2:10, 11).

Christianity is based on God's revelation. Rejecting that, a society will gravitate to either of the dangerous extremes of rationalism on the one hand, believing only that which we can understand, or mysticism on the other, denying that there is objective truth.

We must have God's infallible guidance to understand the spiritual world. We have no basis to assume that it is simply a logical extension of that which we perceive in the natural world. Thus, rationalism and mysticism are untenable. We need God's revelation to subsist both in time and in eternity. We must bow to the authority of the Bible even when we cannot understand either it or the circumstances taking place around us.

God's Word Revealed—Inspiration

Another important term in a discussion of God's communication of truth is "inspiration." Paul specified that the Spirit of God transmitted God's truth to the authors of Scripture (2:12). The Lord Jesus had predicted this: "But the Comforter, which is the Holy Ghost, whom the Father will send in my name, he shall teach you all things, and bring all things to your remembrance, whatsoever I have said unto you" (John 14:26).

Each writer of Scripture, including Paul, was guided by the Holy Spirit to select the very words God wanted to be included in the Bible. The Holy Spirit did not allow the writers to put anything into the 66 books of the Bible that God wanted left out, and He did not allow the writers to leave anything out that God wanted in.

The content of Scripture was "not in the words which man's wisdom teacheth, but which the Holy Ghost teacheth" (2:13). Notice again that Paul is talking about specific "words." God inspired the exact words of the Bible.

The writers of Scripture had distinct personalities, different vocabulary ranges, and individual writing styles, but they were all borne along ("moved") by the Holy Spirit in the writing of God's Word (2 Peter 1:21).

Liberal theologians regard the Bible as simply a religious book that is inspiring in some respects but neither inspired nor reliable. Neo-orthodox theologians believe the Bible is the product of writers who had encounters with God and shared their insights based on those encounters. They claim a Bible passage becomes the Word of God as it speaks to the reader.

These are false teachings regarding the nature of Scripture. The Bible does not merely become the Word of God; it *is* the Word of God.

Furthermore, it is not a subjective revelation; it is an objective revelation. Its validity does not depend upon the feelings of its readers. Instead of being judged by its readers, it judges its readers.

Biblical theologians are correct in rejecting both the liberal view and the neo-orthodox view in favor of the Bible's own claim that it is God's Word in its entirety. Second Timothy 3:16 states, "All scripture is given by inspiration of God . . . ." Literally, "All scripture is God-breathed."

14. Why is it important for us to understand the nature of inspiration?

The term verbal inspiration, as we have seen, means that all the words of Scripture are inspired. Plenary inspiration means the Bible is inspired in all its parts. Because the whole Bible is the inspired Word of God, it is authoritative, inerrant, infallible, and reliable.

God's Word Revealed—Illumination

15. Read 1 Corinthians 2:14–16. How does a person's spiritual standing relate to his or her ability to understand the Scriptures?

Because fallen man is spiritually dead, he cannot comprehend spiritual truth (2:14). However, the born-again person—"he that is spiritual" (2:15)—can discern spiritual truth.

16. How would you respond to a believer who says he doesn't read the Bible because he doesn't understand it?

Paul states in summary: "We have the mind of Christ" (2:16). As we study God's Word, the Holy Spirit opens the eyes of our understanding.

Making It Personal

17. As you go about your life how reliant are you on the wisdom of God's Word to deal with situations that arise?

18. What does your level of reliance on God's Word say about how profitable you actually think it is?

19. How have you shared God's Word with an unbeliever recently?

20. What are some ways you could use Scripture in witnessing to the unsaved?

21. With whom will you share the gospel this week?

22. Memorize 1 Corinthians 2:4 and 5.

The Church's One Foundation

God expects believers to serve Him with proper motives.

1 Corinthians 3

"For we are labourers together with God: ye are God's husbandry, ye are God's building" (1 Corinthians 3:9).

A church census taker asked a resident, "What's your church preference?"

"Red brick colonial," the resident replied, obviously focused on some of the least consequential descriptions of a church.

Hopefully you would express your church preference in a different way. You might say you preferred a church of loving, growing, fruitful Christians rather than a church of Bible-ignoring, back-stabbing Christians.

Getting Started

1. If someone asked for your church preference, what would you say?

2. What would you include in a list of your favorite qualities in a church?

Carnal Babies

Paul told the Corinthian Christians they were "carnal" (3:1). In doing so, he used the word meaning "of the flesh." In other words, they were acting in a similar fashion to people who were not born again. The energy for their works was derived from the flesh, or sin nature, the same source as that which fuels the unbeliever (cf. Rom. 8:9, 12, 13). As Paul goes on to show, living in this fashion as a Christian will ultimately have devastating consequences for eternity.

3. Read John 3:5, 6. What two categories of people are identified in these verses?

4. What does Paul imply by his use of the word "babes" in verse 1?

Paul had to communicate basic spiritual principles to the Corinthian believers because they could not digest anything stronger (3:2). There is nothing abnormal about babyhood, but if it lasts five years or longer it is certainly not normal.

5. How does a five-year-old's knowledge and behavior differ from a baby's knowledge and behavior?

6. How should the knowledge and behavior of a Christian, five years old in the Lord, differ from the knowledge and behavior of a new convert?

The Corinthians actually had two related problems, disobedience and immaturity (3:1). To be "spiritual" is to "walk...after the Spirit" (Rom. 8:1). This does not necessarily speak to the issue of maturity. A person could be "spiritual" although a "babe" (cf. 1 Pet. 2:2). To state it another way, all "carnal" Christians are "babes," but not all "babes" are "carnal." The need of "babes" is to mature. The need of "carnal" Christians is to become "spiritual."

The Corinthians sinned against the knowledge that Paul had imparted to them in his year and a half of personal ministry among them (cf. Acts 18:11). What an opportunity they had to grow and serve. Yet many of them squandered it.

Carnal Bickerers

The Corinthian Christians' carnality was evident not only in their lack of spiritual knowledge and growth but also in their bickering. Paul indicted them for their carnality, charging: "There is among you envying, and strife, and divisions, are ye not carnal, and walk as men?" (3:3). The Corinthians formed factions around personalities. Some screamed, "We follow Paul!" Others shouted, "Apollos is our man!" However, it seems no one was exclaiming, "We are all one in Christ!"

Corinthian carnality did not end in the first century. It can be seen often in churches today. Here is an illustration: Some church members line up behind Deacon X in opposition to Deacon Y and his followers. Another group supports Mr. Z in calling for the resignations of both Deacon X and Deacon Y. Before long, the whole church is engaged in a nasty fight. Friendships splinter, feelings spill out, and faith splatters while the church splits. In customary fashion, the Sunday morning congregation sings beautiful songs about love and unity, but at the Wednesday night business meeting the members' true attitudes and motives rise to the surface. Meanwhile, the community looks on as the church's testimony is destroyed from within.

7. Read Ephesians 4:3. What can Christians do to safeguard church unity?

8. What should you do if a fellow church member approaches you with speech that is meant to engender strife?

Biblical churches are susceptible to the very sins that gripped the church at Corinth. A Biblical church promotes an environment where Christians desire to stay connected to one another in close fellowship and use their spiritual gifts to serve one another (cf. 1 Cor. 1:7). These good things, however, can be misused and abused. Relationships can become strained over things that seem insignificant, and groups that were aligned together for good causes can suddenly turn on one another. We must pray for the Godly unity of our churches and always be on the lookout lest envy, divisions, and strife enter the congregation.

Church Involved in Construction

Paul now turns to a very positive and motivational illustration that he offers this carnal church. Paul also skillfully weaves a dire warning into the offer that he presents.

The illustration is based on the idea that a building project demands teamwork. Architects, engineers, contractors, foremen, and crew members must cooperate, each contributing his skills where they will do the most good. Not one of them has the freedom to make major decisions or act independently without informing the others. A rogue decision maker jeopardizes the success of the entire project and the safety of the workers.

In the remainder of 1 Corinthians 3, Paul informed the Corinthian Christians that they were involved in a building project. They each had something important to contribute, and each was accountable to the others for his or her portion of the work.

Building on the Right Foundation

Before alluding to Christian service as a building project, Paul referred to himself and Apollos as workers in God's field. They were simply the human instruments God had used to prepare a spiritual harvest in Corinth (3:5). Paul had planted the gospel seed; Apollos had watered it; but God made it grow (3:6).

9. Read 1 Corinthians 3:7. How do the "workers in God's field" compare to God?

Paul and Apollos had worked as one. They were a team, and both of them would receive rewards for faithful service (3:8). Paul assured the Corinthian believers that he and Apollos were coworkers with God, and the Corinthians were the field in which they labored for God (3:9a).

10. In your church, how do the tasks of planting and watering get done?

11. In light of Paul's comments in 3:6, how might your church need to change its view of evangelism?

Switching to a building metaphor in 3:9, Paul compared the Corinthian church to a building. "Ye are God's building," he wrote.

Notice that the Sovereign Lord owns both the field and the building. Both are His properties. They exist to bring Him glory and He expects them to be productive and useful.

The stability of a church's ministry depends upon its foundation. If it is built on the Rock, Christ Jesus, it will endure and enjoy God's blessing. If it is built on man, it will fail.

12. How would one know if a church is anchored to Christ as its foundation?

13. How can a church attain stability in Christ?

Paul told the Corinthians that he and other Christian leaders were simply builders, but Jesus Christ was the Church's foundation (3:10). Paul had laid the foundation by introducing Christ to the Corinthians (cf. Rom. 15:20). Christ alone is the foundation upon which the Christian can rest his salvation and a life of service (3:11). And once confident that his life is set upon that foundation, a believer's potential for service and growth is virtually limitless. Paul counsels us to utilize wisdom in building a glorious superstructure that will rise high above the foundation.

Building with the Right Materials

How would you like to pay a fortune for a house constructed of cheap, flimsy, flammable materials? You would not, because you know the house would not outlast the mortgage. Paul emphasized the importance of using the right quality of materials in building a life and ministry. A Christian can build with "gold, silver, precious stones" or with "wood, hay, stubble" (3:12). The first class of materials is valuable; the second is inferior. The first endures; the second expires.

Paul is talking specifically about the Corinthian church ("God's building," 3:9) being further built up by its members. Each member would be judged based on their individual contributions. By way of application, we may consider that each of us as believers have the opportunity to build our own "building," i.e., our own individual life of service to the Lord (cf. Matt. 7:24–27). Let us build skillfully with the utmost care.

14. How much attention do you give to what "building materials" you are using while in your Christian service?

A Christian's works will be inspected at the Judgment Seat of Christ (3:13; 2 Cor. 5:10). The penetrating gaze of Christ, whose eyes are "as a flame of fire" (Rev. 1:14b), will examine those works. If they fail to meet His standards, they will be burned up. If they pass, then they will endure and the Christian will be rewarded (1 Cor. 3:14, 15).

Notice that Paul anticipated that all Corinthian church members would be present for the Judgment Seat of Christ—even if their works could not be rewarded. This reinforces the general New Testament teaching of a regenerate church membership; a local church is to admit into membership and consist of only those with a testimony of salvation by grace through faith in Jesus.

It is important to know that the Christians who "suffer loss" (3:15) at the Judgment Seat of Christ do not lose their salvation. Paul assured: "If any man's work shall be burned...he himself shall be saved; yet so as by fire" (3:15). Salvation does not depend upon our record of service but on the Savior's redeeming grace. Our sins were judged at Calvary; our service will be judged at Christ's Judgment Seat.

15. Is it possible to perform Christian service in a sinful way? Explain.

16. What are some wrong motives a believer might have for serving the Lord?

Right Motive: To Receive a Reward

A small quantity of gold, silver, and precious stones carries more value than a large quantity of wood, hay, and stubble. A ton of hay sells for less than an ounce of gold. Stubble is completely worthless. Obviously, rewards are based on the value of our works instead of the vastness of our works. It is better to do a few things faithfully and well for the Lord's glory than to do many things for our own glory. Even little acts of service prompted by the Spirit will be rewarded, whereas big, showy deeds performed in the flesh will suffer loss (cf. 1 Cor. 4:1–5; Gal. 6:7–9).

17. Read 1 Corinthians 9:25; 1 Thessalonians 2:19, 20; 2 Timothy 4:7, 8; James 1:12; 1 Peter 5:4. What rewards are mentioned in these verses?

Let us not miss the impact of this profound illustration that Paul uses. By building on the glorious foundation of Jesus Christ, we may construct out of our lives a sparkling tower that will shine through the darkness of this world, emblazoned with the reflective glory of eternity.

Right Motive: To Please the Resident

The Holy Spirit resides in Christians. Paul told the Corinthian believers, "Know ye not that ye are the temple of God, and that the Spirit of God dwelleth in you?" (1 Cor. 3:16). By fighting and politicking in the church, certain Corinthians were destroying God's temple, that holy dwelling of the Spirit (3:17). Paul warned that they would feel God's hand of judgment on them.

Greek philosophy taught that the body was of little value and therefore could be spent on wanton pleasures. Paul, by inspiration, taught that the body of the Christian is the very temple of the Spirit of Lord. As such, it is to be maintained with care and used only for holy purposes. Paul will deal with this subject again in 1 Corinthians 6:19 and 20.

Right Motive: To Honor the Owner

Christian workers must recognize that the church is also God's temple.

This actually seems to be Paul's emphasis here (cf. Eph. 2:21; 1 Pet. 2:5).

His people belong to Him, and He cares about them. Occasionally, a church leader may think and act as if he owns the church. He may order God's people to do what he says and may threaten to split the church when he does not get his way. God will deal with such a person in no uncertain terms.

Christians who cause divisions in a church demonstrate that they are no wiser than the unsaved (3:18, 19). Moreover, it is foolish to attempt to build the church using human wisdom. A fool glories in himself or in other human beings, but such glorying displeases the Lord (3:20, 21a).

Instead of seeking to establish a following, the Christian should thank God for all the Christian leaders He has provided for the edification of the whole body (3:21b, 22). After all, Christian leaders are not gods; they are simply gifts from God among His other gifts (3:22). All of us belong to Christ, and Christ belongs to God (3:23). Furthermore, a Christian leader can be effective only to the degree that he is anchored upon Christ and His Word.

18. What is the difference between respecting a pastor and reverencing him?

The thought of a wrecking ball smashing against a church building is not a pleasant one The scene floods the mind with images of a church once alive with singing, preaching, praying, and happy conversations. How stark the contrast between those images and that of the church under demolition! What led to that church's closing and deterioration? Who destroyed the church's life before the wrecking ball destroyed its walls? How could it have been prevented?

What a pleasant sight, though, to see a crane hoist trusses into place for a new church building! Images of future joyful worship, happy fellowship, and productive service come to mind.

In your church, you can work like wrecking balls or cranes. The choice is clear. Man the cranes!

Making It Personal

19. How will you become more careful about the spiritual construction and maintenance of your life?

20. What wrong motives have you had for serving God?

21. Which of the good motives for serving God will you allow to direct your service for God this week?

22. Memorize 1 Corinthians 3:9.

Just Be Faithful!

The believer is to be a faithful servant of God.

1 Corinthians 4

"Moreover it is required in stewards, that a man be found faithful" (1 Corinthians 4:2).

A television show asked the public to help police locate a fugitive. As the scenario unraveled, the audience learned about a woman who had stolen large sums of money from department stores. In each case, she had been hired as a bookkeeper. Her diligence and dependability soon gave her model-employee status. Eventually she was trusted with the task of collecting end-of-day receipts from all the cash registers and depositing them in the store's safe. One night when she was alone in the store, she walked away with all the cash receipts. The model employee was not such a model after all. In the final analysis, she was untrustworthy and unfaithful.

Getting Started

1. How are others counting on you to be reliable in specific aspects of life?

2. How important to you is the faithfulness of others?

God expects us to be faithful in our service for Him. But unlike the employee in the example, our faithfulness should prove to be genuine.

Searching the Scriptures

Although Paul held the high office of apostle, he was humble. He recognized how much he owed to the grace of God, and he understood the principle of accountability.

Principle of Accountability

Referring to himself and other preachers such as Apollos and Peter, Paul wrote: "Let a man so account of us, as of the ministers of Christ, and stewards of the mysteries of God" (4:1).

The Greek word for "ministers" in 1 Corinthians 4:1 is *huperetes*, meaning under-rowers. An under-rower was a reviled slave aboard a ship. Working at the bottom level of the ship, he manned a set of oars and rowed hard as the pilot barked commands. One can only imagine the difficulties, discomfort, and dishonor that accompanied such a role.

3. How does the meaning of the word "ministers" help you see the importance of being faithful?

4. How does it help you understand the level of commitment that being faithful demands?

A "steward" (4:1) in an ancient household functioned as its manager. As a wise servant, he made the best possible use of everything the owner placed in his custody. He was personnel manager, paymaster, purchasing agent, and treasurer.

God had entrusted Paul and the other apostles with "the mysteries of God" (4:1). God had disclosed to them truths about the gospel, the nature of the church, and the believer's standing in Christ. And God required them to be faithful in handling the truth (4:2). Just as a household steward was accountable to his master for how he managed what was entrusted to him, so Paul and his coworkers were accountable to God for what they did with the great truths He had entrusted to them.

Paul's goal was to faithfully pass on the content and understanding that he had received without making any additions, subtractions, or compromises (cf. 4:6; Acts 20:27; 2 Tim. 2:1, 2). He pressed the Corinthians to follow his example of wholehearted devotion and faithfulness to the truth.

5. What are the characteristics of a minister who is serious about being faithful to the truth?

6. How should being faithful to the truth affect the Sunday School curriculum and other teaching materials a church chooses to use?

We are accountable as God's stewards. Are we faithfully managing what He has given to us, first and foremost in our handling of God's truth?

Verse 2 states that faithfulness is the key characteristic of a godly steward. This means that the steward's current accounts must receive his primary focus. In due time, God may reward the faithful steward with an even greater accountability (cf. Matt. 25:14–30).

7. Read Matthew 25:24–30. What does the Lord's treatment of the man in the parable reveal about the character of God?

Prospect of Approval

Paul was not intimidated by the Corinthians' opinion of him (4:3a). He knew that any human evaluation of his Christian service, including his own evaluation, could be faulty (4:3b).

8. Read 1 Corinthians 4:4. Why is being most concerned about the Lord's judgment an important part of being faithful to the Lord?

Although Paul had a clear conscience (cf. Acts 24:16), he understood that only the Lord could evaluate accurately (1 Cor. 4:4). He longed for his Master's approval at the Judgment Seat of Christ (4:5). In the meantime, any human judgment was bound to be flawed.

Paul taught that possessing a clear conscience does not make the believer blameless before God in terms of the evaluation that Christ will render at His Judgment Seat. This includes the fact that He "will bring to light the hidden things of darkness, and will make manifest the counsels of the hearts" (4:5). In other words, He will judge thoughts and motives that even we ourselves may not have been aware of. It also includes the fact that He will judge us against the entirety of His revealed Word, not just the things that we thought were important or the things we understood.

We may be comforted to know, however, that our mere presence at the Judgment Seat of Christ will mean that we are safe in heaven for eternity. Furthermore, our sins will not be the issue (cf. Heb. 10:17). The Lord will only be examining us with regard to the degree of our reward.

9. How much thought have you given to the rewards that you will receive at the Judgment Seat of Christ?

Although we are encouraged when we hear a word of appreciation for our service, what matters most is the Lord's approval. If He counts us faithful at His Judgment Seat, then we shall be satisfied.

10. On the basis of what you have learned about the church at Corinth, what quality or characteristic might a Corinthian have considered highly desirable in a church leader?

11. Would God consider those qualities important qualities or characteristics? Explain.

Plea for Accord

Although Paul used his name and Apollos's name in his discussion about idolizing spiritual leaders, the teaching had broader application (4:6).

One of the aims that Paul had in writing this letter was to demonstrate the sufficiency of Scripture to the Corinthians. Paul used the examples that he chose "that ye might learn in us not to think...above that which is written."

As Bible believers, this truth hits an area of potential weakness. The temptation to add to Scripture is greater than the temptation to subtract from Scripture. But both errors are equally dangerous (cf. Rev. 22:18, 19). The Corinthians added a loyalty to ministers. This is seen in contrast to the Galatians, who added law-keeping to the Biblical mandates for New Testament believers (cf. Gal. 4:21).

12. Why would a Bible teacher be tempted to add to the Word of God?

Pride and worldly wisdom always lead to self-exaltation or exaltation of others, but no believer deserves personal glory. Instead, a Christian owes everything to God's grace (1 Cor. 4:7). Instead of uniting in one accord as one team under Christ as Lord, the Corinthians divided into a number of teams, each under a different leader. Instead of being of one accord, they were experiencing discord.

In forgetting this truth, the Corinthians' pride and worldly wisdom led them into a focus on materialism. They lived like kings (4:8a) and forgot that the Christian life calls for self-denial and dependence upon God. Perhaps Paul was implying that the Corinthians were living as if they thought that they had begun ruling in the millennial kingdom, even though they had not. This current church age is the season for faithfulness in the midst of opposition. Paul wanted the Corinthians to mature so that they would truly be ready for the time of Christ's reign.

Faithful stewardship acknowledges that God gives to each Christian what He deems best. It fosters a spirit of contentment and leads the believer to commit his money, possessions, time, and abilities to God. Paul wanted the Corinthians to practice such faithful stewardship and to know that true riches are spiritual, not material (4:8b).

Faithfulness in Rigorous Service

Paul shunned fame and followed Christ. Faithfulness was his goal.

Although Paul looked forward to reigning with the Corinthians in Christ's kingdom (4:8), he faced harassment in his ministry. He was a "spectacle unto the world, and to angels, and to men" (4:9).

The apostles were despised, ridiculed, and scorned by the world. They willingly experienced weakness and were considered "fools for Christ's sake," but the Corinthian believers did not want any part of such suffering. They coveted human wisdom, power, and glory (4:10).

13. How is leadership in the spiritual realm different from leadership in business? politics? money? fame?

14. How strongly is your thinking influenced by a worldly model of leadership?

The apostles did not live luxuriously. Paul's apostolic job description in verses 11–13 certainly would not have attracted any financially comfortable or professionally and socially prosperous Corinthians.

15. Read 1 Corinthians 4:11–13. How does Paul's apostolic job description help you understand the degree to which God expects us to be faithful in serving Him?

Faithfulness in Discipleship

16. Read 1 Corinthians 4:14, 15. What motivated Paul to speak to his children in the faith so plainly?

It was Paul who braved the opposition in Corinth on his second missionary journey and spent a year-and-a-half proclaiming the gospel in the wicked city (cf. Acts 18:1–17). Paul thus urged the Corinthians to imitate him. He deployed Timothy to Corinth to help them do so (1 Cor. 4:16, 17). Paul lived such a devoted and godly life he could tell the Corinthians both "Do as I say" and "Do as I do."

Sometimes a son or daughter does not heed their father, so the father has to reinforce his teaching with discipline. Some Christians at Corinth thought that Paul was giving vain threats. They interpreted Timothy's arrival to mean that Paul would never personally intervene in their affairs. So these arrogant, insolent prodigals rebelled against Paul's teachings (4:18). However, Paul assured them that he would visit Corinth and discipline his rebellious children if the Lord willed (4:19). They would learn the hard way that Paul was very serious; he had apostolic power to back up his words with action (4:20).

The Corinthians believed they were already in "the kingdom of God" (4:20). But this was a vain boast. The telling miraculous signs that will accompany the millennial kingdom were absent (cf. Isa. 35; Heb. 6:5).

Like a faithful father, Paul would not withhold discipline when it was necessary. But he preferred to give his spiritual children an opportunity to repent first. So he offered a clear choice: The sinning members of the Corinthian church could continue in their wicked ways or submit to his inspired counsel. If they chose to keep on sinning, Paul would institute discipline among them (4:21a). If they repented, he would leave the "rod" on the shelf and be a loving, gentle father in their midst (4:21b).

17. Why is consistently practicing church discipline so important in helping church members to remain faithful?

A church ought to be a team of cooperative workers, bound together by their love for the Lord and for one another. Team members should not form little teams within the big team, but must rather work together faithfully as a well-disciplined unit to honor Christ. Let's be faithful!

Making It Personal

18. Think of what it would have been like to be an under-rower on a first-century Greek ship. Why do you think Paul used such a vivid illustration of a minister?

19. Have you seen yourself as an "under-rower" in your recent service for God? Explain.

20. What prideful or self-centered attitudes or outlooks might you need to address in your life?

21. The Corinthians thought they were already in the millennial kingdom. From what you have already learned, how will you prepare to rule with Christ in His kingdom?

22. Memorize 1 Corinthians 4:2.

It's a Tough Job, but . . .

*The local church should maintain purity
through church discipline.*

1 Corinthians 5

**"Purge out therefore the old leaven, that ye
may be a new lump, as ye are unleavened. For
even Christ our passover is sacrificed for us" (1
Corinthians 5:7).**

Excessive-compulsive cleaners keep their houses spic and span. One stray piece of lint or a few cookie crumbs are calls to action for such neat-nicks. They cannot sit down for a quiet evening of relaxation unless all the dirt is removed and everything is in its place.

Getting Started

1. How tolerant are you of dirt and dust in your house? Do you have to have your floors vacuumed and your furniture dusted once a day, once a week, once a month, or just when someone comes to visit?

2. Would you ever consider a filthy house as a reason to be proud? Explain.

The Corinthians had a very dirty house in a sense, and they were proud of it. Their "dirt" was sin and their "house" was the church, the body of Christ. In 2 Corinthians 5, Paul dealt with the church's need to purge out the sin by practicing church discipline.

Searching the Scriptures

The Bible presents the gospel so that sinners may be saved. Once saved, a Christian should share the gospel with others. He may do this best by offering a verbal witness supported by a righteous life. Similarly, a church will find it easier to reach the world with the gospel when the conduct of its members compares favorably with Christian profession. Unfortunately, the Corinthian church's walk failed to support its talk. Unchecked sin had blunted its testimony. The situation brought Paul's stern rebuke.

Serious Problem

Paul had addressed one serious problem in the church, the problem of divisiveness. Now, in 1 Corinthians 5, he addresses another insidious problem—immorality.

Corinth was buzzing with gossip about a man in the Corinthian church who had committed fornication with his father's wife—possibly his stepmother. Perhaps he had taken this stepmother as his wife.

Paul underscored the heinousness of the man's sin by stating that it was "not so much as named among the Gentiles" (5:1). Although the Gentiles engaged in immoral conduct, they did not practice the particular sin that this man was engaged in.

How did the Corinthian Christians expect their unsaved neighbors to believe the gospel in the face of such scandalous conduct by a Christian?

3. What affect might a scandal such as this have on the witness of individual believers within a local church?

Paul calls the woman in this scenario "his father's wife" (5:1). Bible students are unsure of the exact nature of this man's sin since Paul did not make it clear. What is clear is that this couple was involved in something that Paul considered to be a public sin of a scandalous nature. Perhaps the relationship began in an immoral fashion, and the fact that it involved this man's "father's wife" only served to magnify the gross sin that was already obvious. Paul does not make it clear that they were ever married, so the entire relationship may have been built on immorality.

4. Why do think that Paul did not give us more specifics?

5. What reactions from non-Christians to immoral behavior by Christians have you encountered?

6. How can a Christian best counter such reactions?

This dreadful sin in their midst should have appalled the Corinthian Christians and compelled them to discipline the offender. Instead, they were "puffed up," or smug and proud, perhaps of their open-minded tolerance of the situation. They should have grieved that immorality had stained their testimony, but they were indifferent. Instead of excommunicating the offender, they had adopted a laissez-faire attitude (5:2).

The Corinthian church showed the same kind of self-sufficiency and complacency that Jesus condemned in addressing the Laodicean church. "I will spue thee out of my mouth," Jesus told the Laodiceans, "because thou sayest, I am rich, and increased with goods, and have need of nothing; and knowest not that thou art wretched, and miserable, and poor, and blind, and naked" (Rev. 3:16b, 17).

7. What do we know about the Corinthian church that helps us understand this reaction?

Some churches only want to portray a positive atmosphere that leaves the worshipers feeling encouraged and upbeat. This is not the proper Biblical balance, however. There is a time for sobriety in the worship of our holy God. Indeed, there is even a time to mourn.

Specific Procedure

Although church discipline is not a pleasant procedure, it is a necessary one. Here the Apostle Paul gave clear directions on how it was supposed to be handled in the Corinthian situation.

Paul tackled the Corinthian scandal because no one in the church seemed willing to do so. As the Corinthian Christians' spiritual father, and with apostolic authority, he passed sentence on the guilty one (1 Cor. 5:3). He had weighed the situation carefully and had decided the church should excommunicate the offender.

Ultimately church discipline is a congregational responsibility. Paul addressed the church, "when ye are gathered together" (5:4). It is not the prerogative of merely the pastor, deacons, or other leaders to discipline sinning church members. The assembled church owns this prerogative and bears the responsibility to act with the authority of the Lord of the church. It does so by applying the clear teachings of Scripture to the situation at hand (cf. Matt. 16:19; John 20:23). The congregation as a whole was to agree on this pronouncement during one of its formal gatherings.

8. What does the congregational responsibility in exercising church discipline imply about individual church members?

9. Read Matthew 18:15–20. What are the 3 steps in church discipline?

10. What makes church discipline so difficult to carry out?

The church at Corinth was supposed to deliver the guilty member "unto Satan for the destruction of the flesh, that the spirit may be saved in the day of the Lord Jesus" (5:5). What does it mean to deliver an offending church member "unto Satan for the destruction of the flesh"?

By voting to remove the man from the church's membership, the church was, in effect, classifying him as an unbeliever who is completely vulnerable to Satan. If the man were actually an unrepentant believer, God may allow Satan to cause him temporal harm as a means of chastening him for his eternal good (cf. Luke 22:31).

How could the church at Corinth execute the command? They were to officially remove the man from church membership.

By excommunicating the offender, the church was consigning him to a period of suffering at the hands of Satan. The excommunicated offender would learn the hard way that sin's fruit is bitter. The lesson might persuade him to repent and seek restoration.

11. Read Galatians 6:1. How does this verse relate to church discipline?

Solemn Principle

Mankind may issue senseless orders, but the Lord has sound reasons for His commands. An underlying principle was involved in the command issued to the Corinthian church in verses 4 and 5.

"Your glorying is not good," Paul informed the church (5:6). Instead of recognizing the evil and destructiveness of the offending church member's flagrant immorality, the Corinthians prided themselves on their assets: knowledge, communication skills, spiritual gifts, etc.

The principle Paul wanted the Corinthian Christians to grasp was this: "A little leaven leaveneth the whole lump" (5:6). Unchecked sin in the life of just one church member can spread through the church. Also, unchecked sin in the life of just one church member may destroy the testimony of the whole church. The unsaved community may perceive the whole church as hypocritical and unholy.

12. Why is yeast's effect on baking bread a good illustration of the effect a sinning believer can have on a church?

13. What harm does one person's immorality inflict on the church?

14. How might a church restore its testimony following a scandal?

Spiritual Purpose

In verse 7 Paul identified the Corinthian Christians as "unleavened." This is what they were in Christ, for positionally all Christians appear righteous to God (2 Cor. 5:21). However, from a practical standpoint, the Corinthian Christians needed to "purge out therefore the old leaven" (1 Cor. 5:7).

Paul was using this Jewish feast as an illustration. The Passover commemorated not only the sparing of Israel's firstborn but also Israel's deliverance from Pharaoh and Egyptian bondage. In commemorating the Passover, each Jewish family conducted a solemn search for leaven in its household. If they found any leaven, they disposed of it. This purging preceded their offering of a Passover lamb in the temple.

The Corinthians, too, had been set free from slavery by a Passover: Christ, the believers' Passover, was sacrificed for them (5:7). How could they tolerate the leaven of sin in their house, knowing that Christ died to redeem them from sin?

15. How is Christ like a Passover lamb?

16. How does the correlation between the Passover and the Christian life help you see the importance of dealing with sin in the church?

Paul urged the Corinthian church to keep on observing the purity related to Passover. The sins of the old life did not belong in the lives of God's redeemed people. Instead of possessing an evil disposition and practicing sin, the believers were summoned to lives of pure motives and integrity. Their daily living was supposed to mirror the truth they proclaimed (5:8).

17. Read 1 Corinthians 5:6–8. What is Paul doing in these verses?

Sensible Practice

Paul had written to the Corinthians before about matters pertaining to godly living. Although the previous writing was not an inspired New Testament letter, Paul referred to it in giving an important injunction.

Do not "company with fornicators," Paul commanded (5:9). To "company" means to mix yourself with. The Corinthian Christians were commanded not to mix socially with those who engaged in immoral sexual conduct. Instead of fellowshipping with an immoral church member, the Corinthians were supposed to exercise church discipline and excommunicate him or her (5:11–13).

In verse 11 Paul enlarged his command to include disassociation from the "covetous," those greedy of gain and eager to take advantage of others; the "idolater," who worships another god; the "railer," who abuses others; the "drunkard"; and the "extortioner," who seizes more than is his.

The Corinthian Christians were not supposed to eat with such wicked persons. This would bar offenders from fellowship at church members' tables at home and the Lord's Table. Of course, once the offenders repented, the church was to restore them to fellowship lovingly and promptly.

Some had misunderstood Paul's previous command. They wondered how they could avoid relationships with unsaved sinners. Paul explained that his prohibition extended only to interpersonal relationships in the church family, among professing Christians. It would be impossible to sever all contact with sinners unless one were to separate himself from the entire world, which is not what Paul intended (5:10).

In 5:12 and 13, Paul reminded his readers that Christians are not responsible for the judging of the unsaved; God will handle that responsibility. However, Christians in a local church are responsible for the disciplining of their own. They ought to remove offenders from the fellowship.

While it is true that a Christian can ruin his own testimony and the testimony of his local church by sinning, it is equally true that God can forgive and restore the repentant one's life. Studying this portion of 1 Corinthians should increase the desire of the wayward child of God to repent and turn to the church, not being fearful that he will be ridiculed and exiled.

Making It Personal

Together you form one body of Christ with the members of your local church. But before worrying about sin in someone else's life, you should consider your own life.

18. Are you tolerating sin in your life? If so, deal with that sin first of all.

19. What are some reasons a church might hesitate to handle a potential church discipline case Biblically?

20. Value church discipline as a deterrent from sin and as an opportunity to draw erring fellow believers back to God. What could your church do to be ready to discipline members when situations arise?

21. Memorize 1 Corinthians 5:7.

Family Matters

Believers should reflect Christian character in their Christian family relationships and in their personal conduct.

1 Corinthians 6

"Do ye not know that the saints shall judge the world? and if the world shall be judged by you, are ye unworthy to judge the smallest matters?" (1 Corinthians 6:2).

A boy and girl raised in an upscale neighborhood outside of Chicago sued their mother, who was divorced from their father. The girl sued for not getting birthday presents and for having to dicker over how much to spend on a dress. The boy sued for getting an inadequate birthday card with no money in it, for being threatened to buckle his seatbelt, and for not getting care packages in college.

The judge threw the case out. Imagine the flood of similar lawsuits if the children had won!

Getting Started

1. Did you ever wish you could take a sibling or perhaps a parent to court when you were growing up? What were the circumstances?

2. How do you think taking a family member to court would have reflected on your family name?

Familial lawsuits are bad for the family name! And living with each other during and after the lawsuit is not too pleasant either.

Paul addressed the Corinthians in a negative context again. They were suing each other and giving the body of Christ in Corinth a bad reputation.

Searching the Scriptures

Quarrels occur in even the most loving families, but they must not be allowed to rip the home apart. They must be resolved so the family can continue to function as a loving unit. In 1 Corinthians 6, Paul addressed the church family at Corinth and provided guidelines for solving internal disputes and sustaining the church family's distinctiveness.

3. Read 1 Corinthians 6:1. Where should church disputes be settled?

4. What would be some benefits of settling church family disputes within the church family?

5. What would be some reasons not to settle church family disputes in a secular court?

Shameful Practice

Lawsuits were common in the Greek culture at Corinth, as they are today. When Corinthians became Christians, however, they gained an opportunity to resolve disputes with one another in a conciliatory and godly manner. Instead of employing this opportunity, they preferred the old system of scratching, gouging, and biting one another, spiritually speaking, in front of unsaved magistrates (6:1; cf. Gal. 5:15). Who would believe such combatants belonged to the same family of believers in Christ?

6. Why are lawsuits so common from a Biblical perspective?

When Jews disputed with one another, they did not drag the matter before Gentile magistrates; they settled their differences either privately or in a synagogue court. Why could the Christians in Corinth not borrow a page from the Jews' book on interpersonal relationships? Were they not able to find wise arbitrators in the church and ask them to resolve the disputes (6:5)? After all, did not the Corinthian church boast about its wisdom?

Notice that Paul is not necessarily chiding the Corinthians for desiring to have bothersome matters resolved; he is challenging the concept of believers asking an unbeliever to adjudicate a dispute between them.

7. Which spiritual gifts are helpful in resolving differences?

Paul reminded the Corinthian church that someday Christians will judge the world and angels (6:2, 3). Thus, they must prepare now to become what they will be then. Why could they not judge members of their own spiritual family? They needed to place their trust in God and His plan for the church, not their rulers' abilities.

Brothers who brought brothers before unsaved judges blemished the church's testimony in Corinth (6:6, 7a). This practice contradicted Jesus' desire that His disciples would be known for their love (John 13:34, 35).

8. Read 1 Corinthians 6:7a. How did Paul describe the Corinthians' practice of taking each other to court?

Selfless Principle

Paul wrote it would ultimately be better to take a loss or to suffer damages than to go to a secular court (6:7). Of course, this may not be an option in every case. But Paul pointed out that the church members were wrongfully acting as the aggressors in the cases at hand (6:8). They were not simply caught up in circumstances beyond their control. Gaining a satisfactory verdict in such instances would mean little when the legal battle injured the church's testimony.

9. Read 1 Corinthians 6:8. What would motivate a believer to "do wrong, and defraud" his brethren?

Paul is not demanding that one Christian who is legitimately harmed by another simply take the loss. He proposes taking the matter before "a wise man" from the church (6:5).

Paul counsels the church to model the practice of justice, mercy, and wisdom as it oversees the internal resolution of any arguments.

Paul is not teaching that human courts are intrinsically evil, for he also wrote that such "powers...are ordained of God" (Rom. 13:1). Also, this passage does not preclude all interaction between Christians and the governmental court system.

Certain issues may require the court's involvement even if a matter concerns only Christian believers. There could also be a situation in which a church or an individual believer attempts to settle a matter following the tenets of this passage only to find that the other party, although a professing Christian, has elevated the dispute before secular authorities. Christians will certainly need the wisdom of God and the assistance of other godly, capable believers whenever they find themselves in any such circumstances.

Should Christians pursue legal channels in some cases; for example, when a fellow believer has committed a crime? This is a very delicate matter that would depend a great deal on the circumstances, perhaps taking into account what might most help that fellow believer. In some cases, however, reporting certain crimes to the authorities may be legally required.

10. Might a situation arise that would damage the church's testimony if the church were to fail to take legal action? Explain.

Reborn People

We Christians may not be as good as we ought to be, but by the grace of God we are not as bad as we used to be. The Corinthian Christians, too, were not as bad as they used to be, but they kept reverting to conduct that was representative of the old, unregenerate life. They needed to show consistently that God was their Father as they bore a resemblance to Him.

Corinthian society teemed with the vilest sinners (6:9, 10). As a matter of fact, some of the Christians had been rescued from such debauchery.

11. Read 1 Corinthians 6:9–11a. How does this passage help you understand the challenges the Corinthian believers faced in the church and in society?

The Lord had reached down into the miry clay, scooped up the new Corinthian believers, washed them from their filth, set them apart to honor and serve Him, and given them a righteous standing in His sight (6:11). They were sanctified in their position before God.

12. Is there any sin that disqualifies a person from being justified?

As God's reborn people, the Corinthian believers were free from sin; however, some must have believed they were free to sin. Paul explained that liberty in Christ does not give a Christian license to sin (6:12). The unsaved residents of Corinth were watching the Christians' behavior and forming judgments about Christianity based on what they observed. This should have persuaded the Corinthian Christians to be careful about what they did. Even in matters having no legal restrictions, they were well-advised to distinguish between behavior that was "lawful" and behavior that was "expedient" (profitable).

According to verse 12, believers should not be enslaved by any habit. Christians must not live as slaves to physical appetites, including gluttony and illicit sexual behavior (6:13).

13. Read 1 Corinthians 6:13. How should the truth that our bodies are for the Lord affect us?

The Lord designed legitimate physical appetites; the body does not exist to serve these appetites but rather to serve the Lord (6:13b). When the body dies, the physical appetites will die with it, but the Lord will raise the body to resurrection life (6:14). We must live in light of this truth.

The body, then, is important to the Lord, and every Christian should dedicate his or her body to the Lord (Rom. 12:1). But the Corinthians understated the importance of the body, being clouded by Greek beliefs that the body was worthless. As will be shown in lesson 12, this even impacted their view of resurrection and gave the impetus to a heresy that was circulating within the church (cf. 1 Cor. 15:12).

Christ came in a human body and received a glorified body after His resurrection from the dead. He will forever possess that glorified body. Any teaching that denigrates the value of the human body is unbiblical.

It makes no sense at all that a believer would defile his body and dishonor the Lord by committing fornication (6:15). Paul reminded the Corinthian Christians that the sexual relationship between a man and a prostitute binds them together as one (6:16, quoting Gen. 2:24). He underscored the profaneness of such wicked conduct by stating categorically that a believer and the Lord are united as one in spirit (1 Cor. 6:17). The only fitting course to follow was to "flee fornication" (6:18). Indulging in fornication, Paul explained, is tantamount to destroying one's own body (cf. Prov. 6:32).

14. What societal problems has sexual permissiveness created?

15. How does sexual purity benefit a person emotionally? physically? spiritually?

Redeemed People

Paul summoned the Corinthian Christians to honor the Lord with their bodies as redeemed people. The Christian's body "is the temple of the Holy Ghost" (1 Cor. 6:19). Wherever he goes, the temple of the Holy Spirit goes. Whatever he does, the temple of the Holy Spirit does. These sobering facts ought to grab our attention and influence our actions. In some communities, a tavern cannot be located within a certain distance from a church. Yet how often does a believer, whose body is the temple of the Holy Spirit, go where the atmosphere is incompatible with Christlike virtues, thoughts, attitudes, and goals? Perhaps we need to rethink our priorities, redefine our interests, reorder our habits, and rearrange our schedules.

Paul called the Corinthians God's purchased possession (6:19, 20).

16. Read 1 Corinthians 6:20. What was the price that was paid to buy the believer?

We are God's purchased possessions. Our lifelong ambition ought to be to glorify God in our bodies and in our spirits (6:20).

As we saw in lesson 1, the pagan Temple of Aphrodite, with its 1,000 priestesses, dominated the religious scene in Corinth. Paul wanted the Corinthian believers to display the temple of God through their very beings in a way that would put Aphrodite in the shadows. What a contrast they would form with the inhabitants of this wicked city by doing so!

17. As the society around us becomes more promiscuous, is it easier or more difficult to live a holy life? Explain.

As God's redeemed people, the Corinthian Christians had received the opportunity to show their unsaved neighbors that Christ did make a difference in their lives. They could have let their lights shine so others would see their good works and glorify their Father in Heaven (Matt. 5:16). Unfortunately, they muffed that opportunity. They condoned sin in their church and then drafted lawsuits against one another. Their light was dulled. The effectiveness of their future witness hinged on their willingness to heed Paul's exhortation to "glorify God in your body, and in your spirit, which are God's" (6:20).

Have you checked your light's wattage recently?

Making It Personal

You will probably not have an occasion to drag a fellow believer into court. But you will face conflicts with fellow believers. Unfortunately we all at times play the roles of prosecutor, judge, and jury in our own minds. We drag our fellow believers into the courts of our minds.

18. Why do we sometimes feel justified in "trying" an offending fellow believer in our own personal courts?

19. Instead of trying fellow believers in the courts of our minds, what should we spend our energy doing?

20. What does the world conclude about Christ by watching your life, especially your interaction with fellow believers?

21. What will you do to strengthen your testimony before the world?

22. Memorize 1 Corinthians 6:2.

Marriage: Knotted or Not?

Whether single or married, the believer should honor and serve the Lord.

1 Corinthians 7

"For he that is called in the Lord, being a servant, is the Lord's freeman: likewise also he that is called, being free, is Christ's servant" (1 Corinthians 7:22).

S peaking tongue in cheek, a person mused, "It has been presumed that in many cases a young woman chooses a husband who reminds her of her father. If this is true, it explains why so many women cry at weddings."

Although marriage receives more than its share of bad publicity, it ought to be the closest and best relationship a man and a woman share.

Getting Started

1. What might make a marriage a positive relationship?

2. What might make a marriage a negative relationship?

Searching the Scriptures

In 1 Corinthians 7, the apostle Paul sanctioned marriage, addressed some marital problems and provided marriage counseling. In the same chapter, he honored singleness as an option in the will of God. So both married and single people can benefit from a careful study of this passage of Scripture.

Principles about Getting Married

An opinion was held in Greek philosophy that the body was inherently bad and should be despised. According to this thinking, physical desires were to be ignored or denied as much as possible. This attitude spawned asceticism, and asceticism spawned celibacy (cf. Col. 2:20–23). In 1 Timothy 4:3, Paul countered the teaching that imposed celibacy on Christians by attributing it to demonic influence. His opening words in 1 Corinthians 7 support the conclusion that marriage is normal and certainly is an option for the Christian.

Most people since the Garden of Eden have been married (cf. Gen. 2:24; Matt. 19:4–6; Eph. 5:31). Although Jesus Himself was never married, He grew up in a loving home (cf. Luke 2:51) and chose to perform His first miracle at a Jewish wedding ceremony, thereby blessing the institution of marriage (cf. John 2:1–11).

Although Paul agreed that celibacy is good (7:1) and later pointed out its advantages (7:29–34), he also regarded marriage as normal. Knowing how immoral Corinth was and understanding that sexual temptation abounded there, he presented marriage as the only honorable intimate relationship between a man and a woman (7:2).

God planned marriage as a close and abiding relationship (Gen. 2:18–25). Paul speaks very candidly about it here, but he is careful to be tactful in his choice of words. There is nothing sensational or provocative in his writing.

3. What are some practical implications of having one's own spouse?

Marriage is not a 50/50 proposition, as some suggest; it is actually a 100/100 relationship. In Paul's description of marriage, a husband gives himself 100 percent to his wife, and she gives herself 100 percent to him. The sexual relationship offers both husband and wife the opportunity to give themselves to each other in a selfless and loving manner.

4. Read 1 Corinthians 7:3. Why is the verb "render" important in this verse?

5. Why is selfishness so destructive in a marriage relationship?

Each partner ought to respect and meet the needs of the other, withholding physical intimacy only by mutual agreement for the purpose of pursuing spiritual concerns (7:3–5a). In order to avoid any temptation to become unfaithful, abstinence must not continue indefinitely (7:5b).

Paul wanted the Corinthian church to understand that his counsel did not command anyone to get married (7:6). In fact, he preferred and recommended singleness (7:7a). However, he recognized the ability to live as a single as a gift from God. If a person does not possess that gift, he or she should not insist upon remaining single for all of life. Every Christian has some gift (7:7b), which he or she ought to accept and develop.

6. What could happen to a single person's effectiveness for God if he views himself as "broken" or incomplete because of his singleness?

7. What is wrong with the notion that getting married will make a person's life complete?

To the widowed and unmarried, Paul recommended the single life but sanctioned marriage for those whose desires made their singleness unworkable (7:8, 9).

Principles about Staying Married

Drawing from a "command" the Lord gave in Matthew 19:5 and 6, Paul instructed believing couples: "Let not the wife depart from her husband" (7:10). He added: "Let not the husband put away his wife" (7:11). If two Christians did divorce, they were to "remain unmarried, or be reconciled."

Many believe that the Lord allowed an exception for divorce based on adultery (Matt. 5:32; 19:9). Jesus was speaking in the context of Jewish marriage customs in those passages, however, making interpretation of those verses more challenging. Thus some believe that even adultery does not give Biblical grounds for divorce today.

Paul certainly instructed here that divorce for any other reason is unacceptable between Christians. In cases where divorce has occurred, reconciliation should be sought if at all possible.

Some of the verses in 1 Corinthians 7 and other contexts that deal with marriage are difficult to interpret. Godly Bible scholars therefore differ in their interpretations. It would be wise to seek guidance from an experienced pastor or trusted Biblical counselor before attempting to apply this passage to a specific marriage counseling situation.

8. Why should believers find it easier than unbelievers to keep their marriages together?

Next, Paul addressed those who were married before trusting in the Savior but whose spouses were still unsaved. Having no command from the Lord to quote, Paul had to give his own counsel, which in this case was divinely inspired. He ruled that a saved husband should not divorce his unsaved wife if she wanted to continue the marriage (7:12).

Similarly, a saved wife should not leave her unsaved husband (7:13). A believer's presence in a home places the unsaved family members in

the favorable position of receiving blessings (7:14). As God pours blessing into the believer's life, some of the blessing spills onto his family
members. If an unsaved spouse insists on filing for divorce, however,
the saved spouse need not contest the action (7:15).

Naturally, a saved spouse would try to keep the unsaved partner
in the marriage, hoping to be able to lead the partner to the Lord; but
there was no way of knowing if this would happen (7:16). Indeed, if a
saved spouse tried to force the unsaved partner to stay in the marriage,
this might lessen the likelihood that the partner would trust in Christ.

9. Read 1 Corinthians 7:16. What should those who are considering
marriage as a good witnessing opportunity learn from Paul's instructions?

10. What could a believing spouse do to reach his unbelieving spouse?

In 7:17–24 Paul instructed the Corinthian believers: ". . . as the Lord
hath called every one, so let him walk. . . . Let every man abide in the same
calling wherein he was called." Those who were married when they became Christians did not have to dissolve their marriages; nor did single Corinthians have to get married because they had become Christians. Because
they were saved, the Corinthians did not have to switch jobs or change
their marital status. Furthermore, they did not have to become uncircum-
cised or circumcised. They were to focus their concern on obeying God.

Principles about Singleness

Offering his advice for singles as one who was trustworthy (7:25), Paul
first addressed single men. Because persecution was increasing, Paul felt it
was best not to marry (7:26, 27b); but in spite of the difficult times, married
persons should stay married (7:27a). Singles would not be committing a sin
if they married, but they could expect additional stress (7:28).

11. Why might a person desire to stay single during persecution?

12. What might be some heartaches a married couple might experience today?

Paul understood the world order was passing away and what Christians accomplished for Christ far outranked earthly values. He knew unmarried Christians could devote more time to Christian service than their married brethren could devote to it. The responsibilities of married life might distract Christians from spiritual pursuits. So it seemed best to recommend singleness (7:29–35). Once again, though, Paul assured the Corinthians that marriage was a viable option. A father was free to give his daughter in marriage, and he was free not to do so (7:36, 37). Paul's personal preference rested with the latter option (7:38), likely because of the distressful times in which he and the Corinthians lived (cf. 7:26). The choice was not a matter of right or wrong but of good and better under first-century conditions.

13. What pressures might singles face today?

14. Do you believe a single Christian has more time than a married Christian to devote to the Lord's service? Why or why not?

15. What might cause people to be discontent with their marital status?

16. What might help them find contentment with their marital status?

Each believer should focus not on his lot in life but on how he is to serve God in it.

Principles about Remarriage

If people would take more time before marriage to consider what they are getting into, they may not be in such a hurry to get out of the marriage later. Getting married is sometimes referred to as "tying the knot"—a permanent knot instead of a slipknot. Marriage is supposed to bind a man and a woman together in a permanent, loving relationship. Ideally, marriage is supposed to last until death and not simply until divorce.

"The wife is bound by the law as long as her husband liveth," Paul wrote (7:39a), echoing the clear truth of Scripture throughout both the Old and New Testaments. But he made it clear that a widow, and by inference a widower, is free to remarry. He counseled: "But if her husband be dead, she is at liberty to be married to whom she will" (7:39).

Widows and widowers face one restriction in remarrying. They may marry "only in the Lord" (7:39). Only as a believer marries another believer can he or she find maximum fulfillment in marriage. As two persons love each other and love the Lord, they enjoy a harmonious relationship that carries them through the tests and strains of life. Their mutual faith enables them to pray together and to claim the promises of God's Word. They discover what it means to be "heirs together of the grace of life" (1 Pet. 3:7). When Christians honor Christ in their marriage, they enjoy the sweetest human relationship this side of Heaven.

As grand as marriage is, for those who have received the gift of singleness, singleness is better. Believing he was Spirit-directed in his writing, Paul counseled: "But she is happier if she so abide, after my judgment: and I think also that I have the Spirit of God" (7:40).

Making It Personal

17. If you are single, what has been the main focus of your life? How much does a desire for a spouse distract you from serving the Lord?

18. What opportunities to serve God will you take advantage of?

19. If you are married, who do you think of first in your marriage, yourself or your wife?

20. What recent instances show your primary focus in your marriage?

21. Evaluate your marriage from a Biblical perspective and make use of Scripturally-based resources to continually grow the quality of your marriage.

22. Memorize 1 Corinthians 7:22.

Lesson 8

Give Me Liberty and Love

Genuine Christian liberty operates within the bounds of love for others and love for God.

1 Corinthians 8—10

"Whether therefore ye eat, or drink, or what-soever ye do, do all to the glory of God" (1 Corinthians 10:31).

Free from the law, Oh happy condition, now I can sin with Jesus' permission!" So goes a twisted version of a classic hymn. Unfortunately, many believers have adopted this outlook for their lives, claiming to be free in Christ to do as they please. When it comes to grey areas, they do what they want without regard for a weaker brother.

Getting Started

1. What is wrong with such an outlook on life?

2. What could be the consequences of such an outlook?

Paul addressed how to address questionable activities on which believers disagree. Following his instructions should strengthen and unify a church.

Searching the Scriptures

The issue of determining who is in the right in a struggle over Christian liberty is not an easy one. First, we must determine if the issue is truly one of liberty or one of righteousness and sin. Then, to fit the Apostle Paul's template, we must determine who is the stronger brother and who is the weaker brother.

Some Christians assume that the person with the most stringent convictions is the stronger brother and the one willing to explore the frontiers of liberty is the weaker brother. But this may not always be the case. Also, sometimes the stronger brother must limit his liberty for the sake of the weaker brother. Yet this is not universally true as we learn from Paul himself in Gal. 2:11–21. When important principles related to the gospel were at stake, Paul willfully violated the extra-Biblical sensitivities of Peter and his Jewish friends.

We need to study 1 Corinthians 8—10 carefully before attempting to apply it too hastily.

Addressing Problems

The Corinthians had written to Paul about a difficult question: Was it right or wrong to eat food that had been sacrificed to idols (8:1a, 4a)? Some of the Corinthian believers reasoned that it did not make a particle of difference if they ate food that had been offered to idols. After all, they knew that the idol gods did not exist. Some of their Christian friends, however, held a different opinion. Having worshiped idols before trusting in Christ as their Savior, these Christians felt that it was wrong to eat meat that had been sacrificed for idols; their consciences would not let them do it.

Obviously, knowledge alone could not solve the problem and unite the church. It merely puffed up some Corinthians (8:1). Thinking they knew much, the Corinthians failed to comprehend how much they still had to learn in skillfully applying that knowledge in their relationships with others (8:2).

3. What temptations might confront someone who has a solid knowledge of the Bible?

In order to understand this entire section, it is essential to recognize the value that Paul placed on the individual conscience. The conscience has often been compared to an alarm system that alerts a person to the fact that a thought or action is violating the standards set for the conscience.

A weak conscience, which Paul discusses in 8:7, 10, and 12, will malfunction by alerting a person to wrongdoing too easily. Paul makes it clear, however, in Romans 14:23, that violating the conscience even in that case is still sin.

A seared conscience is one that no longer works correctly because it has been violated repeatedly (1 Tim. 4:2). Paul wanted to avoid that at any cost in his own life (cf. Acts 24:16).

Every believer should endeavor to strengthen his or her conscience by building it up on the Word of God so that it sounds its alarm only when the person is actually committing a sin.

Since no Christian's conscience is infallible, no one should attempt to force his or her views on another person unless those views are the direct teaching of Scripture (cf. Rom. 14:22). Every Christian, as a believer-priest under Christ (cf. 1 Pet. 2:9), is given the dignity of determining his or her own mind on questionable matters.

This takes us to the heart of the tension in 1 Corinthians 8. What do we do when Christians differ on matters that seem important to them?

4. In addition to reading Scripture, what are some other ways that we can build a strong conscience?

The proud Corinthians needed to learn the importance of love (8:1b). Love for God is essential, and God knows those who love Him (8:3).

The Greeks worshiped numerous false gods, but Paul and the Corinthian believers knew there was only one true God (8:4). Nevertheless, many imaginary gods commanded the pagans' devotion, and demons energized the whole idolatrous religion (8:5; 10:19, 20). Many Christians at Corinth shared Paul's knowledge that the one true God controls everything and created everything by the agency of Jesus Christ (8:6). But these knowledgeable Christians needed to exercise love toward new believers who still imagined the idols were real and therefore could not eat sacrificed food with a clear conscience (8:7).

Since the Corinthian Christians' relationships to God were not affected either by eating food or abstaining from it (8:8), they needed a set of principles to guide their decision with regard to its effects on other believers.

5. The trends today are obviously heading toward a more lenient view of Christianity in everything from dress and entertainment to styles of worship to views on relationships. Are these trends making the church stronger? Explain.

Even if the Bible does not specifically name a questionable activity, we can apply a number of principles in deciding our position on it. Paul encouraged his Corinthian readers first to apply the principle of consideration.

Principle 1: Consideration

Although a believer in Corinth might claim Christian liberty in eating food offered to idols, he was advised by Paul to consider how this would affect weaker Christians (8:9). If a weaker Christian observed him in the act of eating sacrificed food, the weaker brother might "be emboldened to eat" the sacrificed food in violation of his own conscience, which would be sin (8:10).

Although the knowledgeable Christian would not be ensnared by the pagan beliefs and practices associated with the eating of sacrificed foods, the weaker brother, having already violated his conscience, might be tempted to go even further into active disobedience (8:11). The knowledgeable Christian would be sinning against Christ by injuring the weaker brother (8:12). Paul's appeal to the knowledgeable Christians, then, was to be considerate of weaker brothers and control the use of liberty so as to do nothing to deter the spiritual progress of others (8:13).

6. Is a believer with a legalistic approach to Christian living a weak or a strong brother? Why?

7. Describe situations in which Christians today might apply the principle of consideration.

Principle 2: Self-control

In 1 Corinthians 9, Paul uses several illustrations to make one basic point. Self-control, such as is required for a world-class athlete, is key in making the proper display of Christian liberty toward our fellow believers. Put another way, managing Christian liberty through self-control will help the disciplined believer to run like an athlete toward his eternal reward.

Paul begins with a discussion of his apostleship, then moves to the example he set in his ministry as an apostle.

Some Corinthians saw no reason to heed Paul's teachings at all because they did not believe he was an apostle. But Paul carried genuine apostolic credentials, and the Corinthian Christians themselves were evidence that the Lord had blessed his apostolic ministry (9:1, 2). As an apostle, Paul could claim the same liberty and privileges as other Christian workers. He was free to marry and to receive financial support from those to whom he ministered (9:4–14). Nevertheless, for the sake of the gospel, Paul applied the principle of self-control and set aside these privileges (9:12).

Rather than have someone accuse him of preaching only because he was paid to do so, Paul adopted the policy of preaching without pay (9:15, 16). He preached because the Lord had commissioned him to preach. He believed the Lord would supply his needs (9:17, 18).

Paul chose to limit his liberty for at least three reasons: to set an example devoid of criticism (9:12b); to place a check on his own motives to ensure that he would be qualified for heavenly reward (9:17); and to discipline himself from going beyond that which he was actually at liberty to do (9:18b).

8. Why was it so important for Paul to be concerned about the example he presented to the early church?

9. Read 1 Corinthians 9:19–23. What three words would you use to describe Paul's actions in this passage?

Paul ministered with a servant's heart among Jews and Gentiles alike (9:19). Although his Christian liberty had extricated him from the demands of the law, he became as a Jew in order to win Jews to Christ (9:20). Among Gentiles, he lived apart from the Jewish law in order to win Gentiles to Christ (9:21). In a spirit of self-control, he was considerate of all because he wanted to win people to Christ (9:22, 23).

Some have used Paul's summation in 9:22, "I am made all things to all men," as an excuse to employ bizarre behavior that will supposedly enhance the ministry or make it appear culturally relevant to unbelievers. In context, however, Paul is clearly considering limiting his liberty—not extending it—for the sole purpose of proclaiming the gospel (cf. 1 Cor. 2:2).

In fact, Christian liberty functions best within the bounds of self-control. We are not free to do whatever we feel like doing. Knowing this, Paul disciplined himself. Like a dedicated and well-trained runner, he kept his eye on the finish line and the winner's crown (9:24–26).

10. Read 1 Corinthians 9:27. What did Paul's disciplined life preserve?

11. What disciplines strengthen a believer in his walk with the Lord?

Principle 3: Separation

Having raised the sad possibility of becoming disqualified for a reward, Paul reflected upon what had happened to the Israelites who lacked spiritual discipline in Moses' era.

Although God had redeemed all the Israelites from Egypt, directed them in the wilderness, fed them, and given them water from the rock, He overthrew them there (10:1–6). Why? Because they failed to practice self-control in obedience to God. They reveled in golden calf idolatry, and they committed fornication (10:7, 8). Also, the unfaithful Israelites in the wilderness put God to the test and "murmured" that He was unfair. Again God responded with judgment (10:9, 10).

What happened to the Israelites teaches Christians to stay close to God and far from potentially harmful situations (10:11). These Corinthians who felt they could exercise their Christian liberty by participating in the idol feasts were running the risk of falling into sin (10:12). If they fell, they could not blame it on God (10:13). So the wise course of action was to separate from idolatrous situations (10:14).

12. Read 1 Corinthians 10:20. What sobering connection did Paul make in regard to idol worship?

Those of the church who ignored the principle of separation would face the judgment of a jealous God (10:22).

Principle 4: Edification

Apparently, some Christians pushed their liberty to the point where they felt free to do anything. Paul differentiated for them between what is "lawful" and what is "expedient" (profitable) and between what is "lawful" and what will "edify" (10:23). An important guiding principle in deciding a course of action is not, Do I have the right to do this? but, How will this impact someone else? (10:24).

13. Read 1 Corinthians 10:24. How does this verse speak to the idea that we need to be true to who we are and to feel free to express ourselves without any inhibitions?

Principle 5: Conscience

If a believer purchased a cut of meat in a Corinthian butcher shop, he should eat it with a clear conscience and not investigate its origin (10:25). After all, the Lord owns the whole earth, including the food supply (10:26).

Similarly, if a believer sat at a Corinthian's table as a dinner guest, he should not ask where the food came from, but rather eat it with a clear conscience (10:27). However, if the butcher or the host volunteered that the meat had been offered to idols, the believer should not eat lest he set a poor example of indifference to the significance of pagan religious symbols (10:28, 29). If a stronger Christian ignored others' concerns of conscience, his Christian liberty might be interpreted as license to sin.

Any time a believer eats, he must do so in a manner that would cause himself and those around him to "give thanks" (10:30).

Principle 6: Glorifying God

Though Paul has given us some principles that may be complicated both to understand and to practice, he concludes these three chapters with an unmistakably clear command.

14. Read 1 Corinthians 10:31. What does it mean to glorify God?

15. How does the context of this verse affect your understanding of this verse?

In deciding questionable activities, a Christian ought to ask how he can best glorify God (10:31). If his planned course of action would dull his testimony or hurt a fellow believer's walk with the Lord, he would glorify God by relinquishing his liberty out of love for others. If his planned course of action would enhance his testimony and edify a fellow believer, he would glorify God by pursuing it.

This was Paul's consideration for his life and ministry. His goal was to strengthen Christians and to bring non-Christians to Christ (10:33).

Making It Personal

16. What was your attitude toward exercising Christian liberty before you studied 1 Corinthians 8—10?

17. What is your attitude toward Christian liberty as a result of this study?

18. What changes might you need to make in order to practice your Christian liberty within the bounds of love?

19. Consider whether you have been the "weaker" believer in certain situations. Evaluate your convictions in light of the Scriptures.

20. Memorize 1 Corinthians 10:31.

The Church at Worship

*True worship involves obedience to God and
harmony with fellow believers.*

1 Corinthians 11

**"But let a man examine himself, and so let him
eat of that bread, and drink of that cup. For he
that eateth and drinketh unworthily, eateth and
drinketh damnation to himself, not discerning
the Lord's body" (1 Corinthians 11:28, 29).**

When was the last time your church needed a bouncer for a communion service? Hopefully your church never has! Paul wrote to the church at Corinth with instructions on worship. The church was to follow God's plan for order and harmony. Some of the members were getting intoxicated before observing the Lord's Supper. They were disorderly and disrespectful to God and to each other as they chose to exercise their "rights."

Order and harmony are important for your church, too. If you focus primarily on protecting your rights in church, you will undermine God's mission for it.

Getting Started

1. What would you say are your rights at church?

2. What might a strong desire to defend your rights at church do to the overall ministry of the church?

Searching the Scriptures

The worship of God on the Lord's Day in the company of fellow believers in a Bible-believing church should be a highlight in a Christian's week. If God is worshiped "in spirit and in truth" (John 4:24), He is glorified and His people are blessed. These positive factors did not characterize worship in the church at Corinth, however. Harmful attitudes and practices had invaded its worship. Clearly, it was time to restore order.

Paul concluded his comments on the limits of Christian liberty by encouraging the Corinthians to follow his example (11:1). He praised them for remembering him and for holding the teachings he had given them verbally (11:2). The Corinthian church had a good doctrinal foundation, but its deportment left much to be desired. Its beliefs were intact, but its behavior obviously needed correction.

Correction to Order in Worship

Bible students are divided as to the question of whether Paul's words, especially regarding head coverings on women, deal with a local "custom" in Corinth or whether they are to be taken as binding upon "the churches of God" throughout this age (11:16).

In favor of taking this passage as treating a localized custom is the fact that it stands alone in the New Testament in discussing the obscure subject of head coverings. In support of seeing it as binding throughout the church age is the fact that the text does not appear to make local customs a limitation of Paul's commands.

What can we say to all this? It is clear that the women in most of our churches do not wear head coverings to worship. If Paul intended his counsel to apply at all times, his words have been more or less forgotten over the centuries. Even if one takes the view that Paul is commenting on the local situation in Corinth, however, there are still more important points in this section that must be learned and applied.

Paul is speaking here about the distinct roles of men and women in the church.

Today, it is common to find women in careers previously closed to them. Thus, some might think that for the church to differentiate between men and women at all is simply a vestige of a bygone, discriminatory era. But God's Word, not public opinion, sets the standard for behavior in the church. Paul's words here are rooted in the character of God as expressed in His plan for creation. They are not to be dismissed as bigoted ramblings.

In the larger context, we know that Paul's teachings barred women from positions of authority over men in church worship and instruction (cf. 1 Cor. 14:34, 35; 1 Tim. 2:12). Some claim that cultural considerations in the first century were the only grounds for Paul's prohibition. Those who make that claim argue that women then were apparently uneducated and unskilled while women today are as well-educated and as highly skilled as men. They therefore conclude that women can even be ordained for ministry if the women so desire. But Paul's reasoning in this section completely denies such logic.

God is a God of order. Within the Godhead, God the Father is "the head of Christ" (1 Cor. 11:3). In His earthly ministry, Jesus willingly subordinated Himself to the Father, although He and the Father are co-equal, co-eternal, and co-essential. The Father, Son, and Holy Spirit share one divine essence yet have distinct roles.

In the marriage relationship, "the husband is the head of the wife" (Eph. 5:23; cf. 1 Cor. 11:3). This does not give him dictatorial power but a responsibility to provide loving leadership in his marriage to a woman who is of equal value in her person and equal standing before God as a Christian (cf. Gal. 3:28).

Woman is not inferior to man in terms of her nature or character or even in terms of her abilities. Certainly Christ, who ranks under the Father in terms of his role in the Godhead, is not inferior to the Father. The teaching of subordination in 1 Corinthians 11:3 relates to order; it is not a statement about anyone's worth as an individual, nor does it imply a lack of capability.

3. How do the differences between men and women demonstrate the glory and wisdom of God?

4. Is an army sergeant necessarily a better person than a private? Is a company president necessarily a better person than a shipping clerk? Is a husband necessarily a better person than his wife? Why, then, are there levels of authority in the military, in business, and in the home?

A professional woman may wonder why she would need to be under the authority of less-qualified men in the church. The issue is not her worth as a person or her level of knowledge and skill. The issue is God's created order. God, not culture, is the origin of the male and female distinction in the church. And God intends His standards for worship and service to be for His glory (cf. Eph. 3:21; Isa. 55:8, 9).

In his leadership role in the Corinthian church, a man was supposed to pray or prophesy (declare a revelation from God) with his head uncovered. Otherwise, he dishonored his head (11:4). In Corinth, men did not wear veils over their heads, but women did. If a man wore such a covering, it suggested he was abdicating his role as a man and a leader and would disclaim his God-appointed headship of both the woman and earthly creation. It would also be a denial of Christ's authority over him.

Women, on the other hand, wore veils. If a Christian woman prayed or prophesied with her head uncovered, she dishonored her head just "as if she were shaven" (11:5, 6). Her uncovered head would signify she was unwilling to accept her husband's headship (11:7–9). This lack of cooperation with God's order would offend the angels, who were observing the Corinthian assembly with keen interest (11:10; cf. Eph. 3:10; 1 Pet. 1:12). The veil was also a token of modesty. Any woman who chose not to wear a veil was likely to be considered immoral.

5. What principles can we draw from this section regarding the relationship between dress and worship?

Paul felt some might regard the woman as inferior to the man, or that some man might use his teaching about headship to lord it a woman. Therefore, he reminded his readers that the well-being of both man and woman is reliant upon the other. The Lord so ordered His plan for the human race that the Christian man cannot degrade woman without degrading himself, nor is the woman to be detached from the man (11:11, 12).

Paul asked the Corinthians to evaluate this whole matter from two perspectives. First, did it seem proper for a woman to pray with her head uncovered? After all, even by nature it is normal and respectable for a woman to have long hair and a man to have short hair (11:14, 15a). Since God gave woman the natural covering of long hair (11:15b), should she not understand the importance of covering her head when she prayed and prophesied?

Second, Paul did not want to debate this teaching; he simply concluded the matter by stating that neither the apostles nor the churches accommodated any custom that violated this principle of the headship of the man (11:16).

6. How could the public worship services of today's churches better honor God and edify others?

God created the male and female as distinct genders with distinct roles. As the world blurs these distinctions, the church should seek to highlight them all the more to the glory of God. This is the time when bold but gracious men and meek but courageous women should step forward in the church and proclaim the Lord's plan loudly and clearly.

7. On the basis of 11:1–16, how would the Apostle Paul respond to the changes we see in our culture today regarding views of gender?

Prevailing Disorders in Communion

Another area in which Paul had to correct his Corinthian friends was their observance of the Lord's Supper.

8. What does the ordinance of communion represent?

9. Given the seriousness of communion, how carefully should a church monitor how it practices communion?

10. How seriously do you approach communion?

The Corinthian church was guilty of poor manners and poor attitudes at the Lord's Table. One by one, Paul identified and corrected them.

According to verse 17, observance of the Lord's Supper had become a negative experience for a number of reasons. Instead of participating as a united body of believers, the Corinthian Christians were divided (11:18). Paul recognized that schisms are inevitable, but he did not condone them. He did teach, however, that divisions in a church reveal the loyal members. By contrast, troublemakers make the best church members look even better (11:19).

Although the whole church met together in one place for communion (11:20), the whole church was not together in one spirit. Physical unity is no guarantee of spiritual unity.

Generally a meal preceded the Corinthian church's observance of communion (cf. Jude 12). The believers brought food to be shared by all. The well-to-do Christians placed their food on the table, but they indulged without sharing it with their poor brethren. They ate and drank until they were overstuffed and intoxicated (11:21). They were turning their fellowship feasts into replicas of pagan feasts. Such selfish indulgence showed a total disregard for the local church and for fellow Christians who were poor (11:22).

11. How should the Lord's Supper relate to social differences that exist in a local church?

12. Imagine your church's members selfishly gorged themselves and became intoxicated before partaking in communion. How would that change the dynamics of your communion service?

Prescribed Order in Communion

The Lord Jesus instituted the Lord's Supper as an ordinance to be observed by the local church. He did this "the same night in which he was betrayed" (11:23). How inappropriate it was for the Corinthians to turn the occasion of the Lord's Supper into a gluttonous festival.

In the Lord's Supper, the bread symbolizes the body of our Lord that was nailed to the cross and subjected to excruciating pain (11:24). The cup symbolizes His shed blood, the price of our redemption (11:25). The communion service declares Christ's death until He comes to take the church to Heaven (11:26).

The Biblical view of communion is commemoration is the Biblical teaching—namely, that the bread and cup represent the body and blood of Christ. The physical body of Christ is not being multiplied through the observance of communion. Nevertheless, communion should be regarded as a solemn ceremony, and our eating and drinking in this context should be taken as no light matter (11:29).

Prerequisite to Observing Communion

Paul warned of discipline from the hand of God if a Christian partook of the Lord's Supper "unworthily" (11:27). Every participant in the Lord's Supper ought to "examine himself" (11:28). He ought to discern the manner in which he approaches the ordinance and confess his sins to the Lord (cf. 1 John 1:9).

13. Why would a regular observance of the Lord's Supper help a believer in his Christian walk with God?

14. How has regularly observing the Lord's Supper affected your walk with God?

15. How should a church handle distributing the Lord's Supper to visitors?

These Corinthians, who abused the ordinance as an opportunity to feast voraciously, were inviting God's chastening (11:29). Many abusers of the ordinance in the Corinthian church had already been chastened with sickness. In fact, many had died for their profane attitude (11:30).

16. What are some inappropriate attitudes to have at the Lord's Supper?

17. Read 1 Corinthians 11:31, 32. How could you prepare your heart and mind for the ordinance?

The Corinthians needed to be considerate of one another at the fellowship meal preceding the Lord's Supper (11:33). If they could not act responsibly and lovingly, they were well-advised to "eat at home" (11:34).

18. What could your church do to practice unity?

Making It Personal

All of us have equal value in Christ, but we do not all have equal roles. God may move you to aspire to a greater role later, but be sure to enjoy and make the most of the role you have today.

19. How has your fulfillment of your role (support/leadership) affected your worship of God?

20. How can you honor God in the role (support/leadership) He has given you?

21. What do you find when you examine your attitude toward fellow believers? If you harbor any ill will, confess it and forsake it. Do all you can to restore your relationships with your fellow believers.

22. Memorize 1 Corinthians 11:28 and 29.

You Are Gifted

The Christian ought to use his
spiritual gifts in love.

1 Corinthians 12; 13

"And there are differences of administrations, but the same Lord. And there are diversities of operations, but it is the same God which worketh all in all. But the manifestation of the Spirit is given to every man to profit withal" (1 Corinthians 12:5–7).

When a husband gives his wife a new set of pots and pans for Christmas, who really benefits? The husband does, of course. He gets to enjoy all the meals his wife cooks in the pots and pans.

In a similar fashion, a spiritual gift does not ultimately benefit the Christian using the gift. Rather, it becomes his gift to others as he serves faithfully and gives of himself.

Getting Started

1. What gifts have you given that really benefited you more than the receiver of the gift?

2. How were those gifts received?

Searching the Scriptures

The topic of spiritual gifts can be approached from several different angles. It is complicated by the fact that some of the gifts are no longer operative today. Of course, there is disagreement about those gifts that are not in use today, so we must be careful to understand the Biblical teaching on this matter very clearly.

In chapter 12, Paul emphasizes an important correlation between the Holy Spirit and Christians who make up the body of Christ. "Diversities of gifts" originate from "the same Spirit" (12:4), going to the "many members...of that one body" (12:12). These gifts allow the body to function effectively when all the members use their gifts to benefit one another (cf. 12:7).

The Scope of Spiritual Gifts

The Corinthians had asked Paul for more information and clarification about spiritual gifts. Since Paul did not want them to stay in the dark about this important subject, he provided a lengthy answer, which he introduced by stating: "Now concerning spiritual gifts, brethren, I would not have you ignorant" (12:1).

The Corinthian Christians had not been saved long. Formerly, they were heathen, captives led by speechless idols (12:2). By faith in Christ they had escaped the bondage of heathenism, but even as Christians they were not free from the attempts of false teachers to deceive them. These false religionists even asserted that Jesus was "accursed" and devoted to destruction. Paul wanted the Corinthians to know that the Holy Spirit did not empower such people. The spiritual person is taught by the Holy Spirit to proclaim Jesus as Lord (12:3).

This acknowledgement of the lordship of Christ is basic to spirituality. It even affects a Christian's attitude toward the distribution and use of spiritual gifts. The Lord can be trusted to distribute spiritual gifts widely and wisely (12:4).

3. What is the difference between a natural talent and a spiritual gift?

The triune God superintends the distribution, use, and effectiveness of the gifts (12:4b–6). Every Christian has at least one spiritual gift, which he ought to employ profitably for the good of others and the glory of God (12:7).

4. How does the subject of Christian stewardship relate to spiritual gifts?

The Christians at Corinth had received a variety of spiritual gifts. First Corinthians 12:8–10, 28, and 29 list them. Most Bible teachers divide these spiritual gifts into two groups: temporary and permanent. The temporary gifts faded out as the writing of the New Testament neared completion. The permanent gifts continue and are in use today.

There is some disagreement about how to categorize the first three: wisdom, knowledge, and faith. Some believe they are permanent gifts, but most likely they were special temporary gifts to help the church in the earliest stages of its development.

Notice the following descriptions of the gifts.

• Wisdom: A direct understanding of divine mysteries not yet explained in the New Testament.

• Knowledge: Direct spiritual insight into truth not yet revealed in the New Testament.

• Faith: Trust in God for the working of miracles.

Certainly, wisdom, knowledge, and faith are available today to all Christians, but these qualities come through the written Word of God (cf. Rom. 10:17; James 1:5). Before the New Testament was written, they were granted directly.

The miraculous sign gifts were foundational to the Church Age and thus limited to the Apostolic Era. We can be certain that the following gifts that Paul listed were temporary.

- Healing: The miraculous ability to restore health.
- Miracles: Extraordinary divine interventions to authenticate the message of the cross.
- Prophecy: Foretelling the future and telling forth divine truths before they were revealed in the New Testament.
- Discerning of spirits: The supernatural ability to distinguish whether a pronouncement or teaching was of God. This was a special gift before the New Testament was completed. (Today, believers need to discern truth and error on the basis of New Testament teaching.)
- Tongues: The ability to speak in a foreign language without having learned it.
- Interpretation of tongues: The ability to interpret what was spoken in an unfamiliar foreign language.
- Apostles: Men, directly chosen and commissioned by the Lord to preach the gospel; they were also eyewitnesses of Christ's resurrection.
- Prophets: Those appointed by God to announce direct disclosures from God concerning His will.

Paul's list also included gifts that clearly are still in use today.

- Teachers: Those who help others learn God's Word.
- Helps: Service on behalf of others; relieving others of their burdens.
- Governments: Competence in watching over church ministries.

The Source of Spiritual Gifts

The Holy Spirit imparts spiritual gifts to believers as He chooses, and He overlooks no one as He shares them (12:11). Some Christians may have several gifts, but every Christian has at least one. This means that every Christian can contribute to the work of the Lord in a significant way.

5. Read 1 Corinthians 12:11. How should our attitude toward our spiritual gifts be affected by the fact that they come from the Holy Spirit?

The Synergy of Spiritual Gifts

The function of the church has some correlations with the function of a football team. A successful football team must follow the coach's play calling, must accept their assigned roles, must treat all team members as important, must know the goal, must take the game seriously, and must practice and develop their skills.

6. What team positions in a church can you name?

7. What might happen if every member of a church tried to function without regard for the Lord's instructions?

8. What might happen if the church members failed to develop and use their spiritual gifts?

The Corinthian church was supposed to operate like a team. Every member was supposed to employ his spiritual gifts in cooperation with his fellow believers. What was true of Corinth is true of us today.

As Christians, we have been baptized into the Body of Christ by the Holy Spirit (12:12, 13). Paul is speaking here of Spirit baptism, not the act or the significance of water baptism. When a person trusts in Christ during this church age, the Holy Spirit places that person in the Body of Christ and comes to indwell him or her (cf. Matt. 3:11; John 14:17).

The Holy Spirit uses all of these Christians to make the church a multi-equipped body (12:14) prepared by the Spirit of God to serve Christ obediently for the good of others and for God's glory. Each local church is such a body and is divinely outfitted to serve the Lord in its sphere of influence.

9. Why is union with Christ basic to the employment of spiritual gifts?

Paul gives a picturesque description of the various parts of this body in 12:15–26. He shows not only how the different members fit together and why all are necessary, but he also describes the activity of some of the parts. The "eye" must be seeing, the ear must be "hearing," and the nose must be "smelling" (12:17), otherwise the body will be incapacitated.

10. Read 1 Corinthians 12:15–30. Why is there no such thing as an unessential Christian in a church?

11. What gives a sense of worth and dignity to even the least conspicuous ministry in a church?

12. What happens when everyone in the church is using his gifts as God intended (12:25, 26)?

In closing his discussion about the bestowing of spiritual gifts, Paul pointed out that the Corinthians were coveting the best gifts, but he would show them "a more excellent way" (12:31). This is described in chapter 13.

Love, the Best Spiritual Gift

The greatest gift imparted by the Holy Spirit to every believer in one sense is agape love, a self-sacrificing, Christlike love (cf. Rom. 5:8). Paul continues his discussion of the use of spiritual gifts in chapter 13, a chapter that we often wrench from its context because of its poetic beauty. Paul is actually giving us the proper motivation and mindset in using our gifts.

A team may be loaded with talent, but if it is wracked by dissension, it will likely encounter a losing season. Bickering, jealousy, grudges, pride, and bitterness can turn even the best equipped team into a dismal failure. Team spirit involves mutual respect and caring. In a church, love for the Lord and one another knits hearts together in ministry. Love guides a team of believers in the right use of their spiritual gifts.

The Corinthian church set a high value on oratory (cf. 2:1). Perhaps this is why the gift of tongues ranked at the top of their list of coveted spiritual gifts. However, Paul informed them that even gilded oratory, delivered without love, was no better than the harsh sounds of "sounding brass, or a tinkling cymbal" (13:1). The gifts of prophecy, knowledge, and faith were also ineffective without the added dimension of love (13:2). Even the gift of giving, demonstrated in the surrender of possessions and life itself for the sake of others, was worthless without love (13:3). Such a sacrifice would not yield the full potential of eternal rewards.

13. What might motivate a person to serve without love?

14. Read 1 Corinthians 13:4–7. How could these qualities be demonstrated in practical ways in a Christian's life?

In the process of giving us this beautiful treatise on the character and importance of love, Paul also gives significant doctrinal teaching on the nature of the miraculous sign gifts that were intended only for the apostolic phase of the church age.

Using a word that describes a leaf falling from a tree and dying on the ground, Paul wrote that love never "fails" (13:8a). It will endure long after prophecies have failed, tongues have ceased, and knowledge has vanished away (13:8b). Tongues would cease because the written New Testament would fully validate the Christian message. Incomplete knowledge of God and incomplete preaching about spiritual truth would be done away upon the arrival of "that which is perfect" (13:10).

It is important to keep in mind here that Paul is writing to church age saints regarding gifts given to the body of Christ within the context of their relationship to that body. Thus, for instance, the fact that there will be a gift of prophecy in operation during the tribulation (cf. Rev. 11:3) is not in view in this discussion. The miraculous gifts Paul is talking about are those that were used to demonstrate the authenticity of the New Testament while also serving as the vehicle of its new revelations.

At some point related to the church age, prophecy would fail, tongues would cease, and knowledge would vanish away. But according to 13:13, faith, hope, and love would abide, or remain. Yet it is exclusively during this life that believers exercise faith and hope. Love is the single one of these qualities that will endure in our eternal relationship with Christ.

Paul insists on the continuation of faith and hope past the conclusion of these miraculous sign gifts, so prophecy would fail, tongues would cease, and knowledge would vanish away before the Rapture would occur.

Paul was referring to the final, written form of God's revelation when he used the phrase, "that which is perfect" (13:10; cf. Rev. 22:18, 19). This is evident from the fact that the "perfect" entity in view here is shown to be superior to its counterpart, "that which is in part" (13:10), namely the ability that the miraculous sign gifts gave to "know in part" and "prophesy in part" (13:9).

"That which is perfect" and "that which is in part" must both be forms of God's special revelation (13:10). Truly, "all the counsel of God" (Acts 20:27) is readily accessible in His "perfect" revelation in Holy Scripture (cf. 2 Tim. 3:16, 17; 2 Pet. 1:3). Compared to it, even the supernatural gifts of prophecies, tongues, and knowledge fade into oblivion.

15. If you really believe the Bible is God's perfect revelation, how should that belief affect your life?

16. Read 1 Corinthians 13:13. How should you respond to the fact that love never fails?

In one sense, love is God's "greatest" eternal gift to His people. It is greater than even faith and hope (13:13). Faith accepts God's offer of salvation and all His promises. Hope anticipates the goal of salvation and the fulfillment of God's promises. Yet faith and hope are unnecessary in Heaven. Love, however, continues throughout eternity. We will love God eternally for Who He is and for what He has done for us by grace.

Spiritually gifted Christians today can bring a little bit of Heaven into their service for Christ by employing their gifts in love!

Making It Personal

17. How seriously should we respond to those who claim new revelation through a miraculous gift like speaking in tongues?

18. How will you respond to the fact that the Bible is complete and sufficient?

19. What have you learned in this lesson that will help you exercise your spiritual gifts toward others with greater love, knowledge, focus, and motivation?

20. Memorize 1 Corinthians 12:5–7.

Tongues Talk

A church should declare God's truth clearly and in an orderly manner and for the edification of its members.

1 Corinthians 14

"Even so ye, forasmuch as ye are zealous of spiritual gifts, seek that ye may excel to the edifying of the church" (1 Corinthians 14:12).

What Bible version does your church use? Do you have a contemporary or a traditional worship service?"

These are two of the most common questions people want answered before visiting a new church. As a result, worship has become a very popular subject among church leaders. The topic invokes many different ideas and emotions if it is not controlled Biblically. First Corinthians 14 is the major passage in the New Testament to guide us through the whole area of offering worship that the Lord of the Church will find acceptable.

Getting Started

1. What elements should a church service include if it is to make an orderly presentation of the worship of God?

2. Should thought be put into the planning of the worship service? Explain.

Searching the Scriptures

Although the gift of tongues was a valid spiritual gift for the Corinthians at this infancy stage of the church, they overemphasized its importance and misused it. Paul addressed these abuses in 1 Corinthians 14.

This chapter is incredibly complicated, and faithful commentators will differ in their understandings of many of its numerous details. That being said, however, some of its most important points are also exceedingly clear. They serve to guide the church today, long after the sign gifts given to the apostles have "vanish(ed) away" (13:8). The key verses that should direct us today are 14:26, 33, and 40.

Prophecy: A Priority Gift

No matter what spiritual gifts the Corinthians had, they needed to exercise them in love. "Follow after charity (love)," Paul advised. He continued, "And desire spiritual gifts, but rather that ye may prophesy" (1 Cor. 14:1). It was wrong for individuals to covet the most visible gifts, but it was not wrong for the church to desire spiritual gifts. The Corinthians placed an undue emphasis on tongues, for example, but Paul cited a more important gift.

3. What does a godly desire for spiritual gifts reveal about a believer?

4. Read 1 Corinthians 3:3. What fact about the church at Corinth proved tongues was not a sign of spirituality?

Of all the spiritual gifts, Paul gave priority to prophecy (14:1). This was the gift of sharing new revelation, including both the foretelling of future events and the telling forth of God's message, which ultimately would be written in the form of the New Testament.

Paul then compared the gift of tongues and the gift of prophecy. Paul contended that if someone spoke a foreign language no one in the congregation understood, he might declare wonderful truths about God's grace, but only God would understand (14:2).

It was far better, therefore, to prophesy since both tongues and prophecy involved giving new revelation. Prophecy, however, would be given in the language of both the speaker and the listeners, whereas tongues would include the added miracle of the speaker using an unlearned foreign language, normally for the sake of the hearers. Such was presumably not always even necessary when the Corinthian church gathered for worship. They were simply fascinated with the supernatural aspects of the gift.

5. Why do you think that some Christians today are fascinated with speaking in tongues?

Paul told the church that declarations of truth delivered in familiar language would build up the listeners in the faith. It would also encourage and comfort them (14:3). That is what was needed desperately in the Corinthian assembly.

6. What do Jesus' discourses reveal about effective communication?

7. Read 1 Corinthians 14:4. What was Paul's main concern here?

Paul compared the results of exercising tongues and prophecy. The speaker of an unfamiliar language profited, but no one else did because no one understood what the speaker said (14:4a). The speaker who prophesied edified the whole church (14:4b).

Notice that Paul was not opposed to the proper exercising of tongues in the Corinthian church at this early stage of church history before Scripture was complete (cf. 13:10). The gift had much to offer if an interpretation of the foreign language made it understandable (14:5).

In verse 6 Paul pointed out how foolish it would be to visit the Corinthian church and speak in an unfamiliar language. His visit would profit the church if he spoke by revelation, by knowledge, by prophesying, or by doctrine. The prophet declared revelation (truth disclosed from God) and the teacher declared what he knew. In either case, the congregation would be edified only by hearing the communication in language it understood. To clarify his point, Paul gave two illustrations.

Paul's Illustrations

If a wind instrument or a stringed instrument provided notes without variation of pitch and rhythm, the so-called music would not make any sense (14:7). An audience would not be moved by the music to be joyful or sad, melancholy or merry. Also, if a soldier blew an unfamiliar trumpet signal, no one in the army would prepare to go to battle (14:8).

Similarly, no one in the church would understand a speaker's message if he spoke in an unfamiliar language (14:9).

Thousands of languages exist in the world, and each makes sense to those who speak it (14:10). Paul told the Corinthians that two persons, each speaking a language the other did not know, would sound like barbarians to each other if they did not understand each other's languages (14:11). Instead of speaking to the congregation in an unfamiliar language, the Corinthians were advised by Paul to desire spiritual gifts that would enable them to edify one another (14:12).

8. What could be some results of believers using spiritual gifts to promote themselves?

9. How might a goal of edifying other believers affect how a believer uses his or her gifts in the church?

Paul believed worship should be intelligent and not simply emotional. There was no point in praying, praising, or preaching in church in an unfamiliar language if no interpreter was present.

Interpretation

Paul bound understanding and emotion together as essential elements of worship (14:13, 14). Only as people understood what was said could they add their "Amen" to it (14:16, 17). Although Paul spoke several languages, he preferred to speak five words in a language his audience understood instead of 10,000 in a language they did not understand (14:19). He urged the Corinthians to consider that the purpose behind the gift of tongues was to demonstrate to the Jewish people that God was validating the gospel (14:20–22a; cf. 1:22; Matt. 12:39). The purpose of prophesying, however, was to benefit believers (14:22b).

Why do we not need to have the sign of speaking in tongues today? We have the completed Scriptures, which bear witness to themselves (cf. Luke 16:31).

Paul suggested that unbelieving Gentiles and Jews alike would be greatly offended if they attended a church service in which the Corinthians spoke in unfamiliar languages (14:23). They would think that Christians were crazy! However, if an unbeliever heard and understood the congregation proclaim God's Word, he would come under conviction, brought about by the whole congregation, and he would see his sins and might turn to God (14:24, 25).

10. How might a congregation convict an unsaved visitor and help him trust in Christ as Savior?

Apparently, the Corinthian worship service was very unruly. Many wanted to contribute, but no one wanted to wait his turn to do so. Paul instructed, "Let all things be done unto edifying" (14:26). We may rightly infer from Paul's inspired counsel that the church was to begin planning its services so that the beneficial aspects of these elements could be presented in a logical and orderly way for the benefit of the entire assembly. The congregation surely must have included some capable people, but the manner in which they were participating was making a mockery of the message they were trying to convey.

The situation in Corinth also required placing restrictions on the use of tongues. When tongues were in operation, the inspired rule was that no more than two or three should speak in tongues in any service, and then only with the assistance of an interpreter (14:27, 28). Otherwise, the person with the gift of tongues was to remain silent.

Revelation

Even prophets needed to follow an orderly procedure. Two or three could speak in a service, and their words were to be evaluated by others (14:29). Most likely, the evaluators were those with the gift of "discerning of spirits" (12:10). They were to act as checks on the person claiming to be a prophet and his assertion to be offering new revelation. This was vitally important, as shown from the fact that if someone received a new revelation, his prophesying had precedence over the prophesying of previously revealed truth (14:30).

Furthermore, the prophets were required to take turns prophesying (14:31), and every prophet was supposed to use self-control. Again, the goal was for the congregation to "learn" and "be comforted" (14:31).

11. Read 1 Corinthians 14:31–33. Do you think a prescribed order of service helps or hinders a church's goal to edify believers? Explain.

Paul's entire focus is encapsulated in 14:33. The Lord's peace must be the theme that underlies all worship. It should contain no hint of confusion. If a reasonable person has to walk away from a church service, a pastor's sermon, or a Sunday School class wondering about its intent, there was something seriously flawed with the presentation. Even at this time of ongoing revelation, Paul demanded orderly worship services.

12. What could your church do to promote orderly worship?

One application of this principle concerned the women in the congregation. If they had questions about what was taught by the prophets, they were not to interrupt the service but were instead to wait until they could ask their husbands at home (14:34, 35). Of course, this injunction required husbands to be competent learners of God's Word!

Paul's teaching regarding the role of women in the Corinthian church may not be as sweeping as it first seems here. He is primarily addressing the specific issue of women being involved in prophesying and speaking in tongues in a church setting, that is "to speak (authoritatively) in the church" (13:35; cf. 11:2–16; 1 Tim. 2:11, 12). The modern equivalent of this would be preaching to the congregation. Paul is not demanding total silence from women.

Since the Corinthians had not originated the Scriptures, they had no right to place themselves above the Scriptures. Their responsibility was to obey the Scriptures. If anyone failed to recognize the Lord's authority in Paul's writing, he would just have to be considered ignorant (14:36–38).

In conclusion, Paul exhorted the Corinthian church to elevate the value of prophecy above tongues without despising the legitimate use of the gift of tongues (14:39). They were to worship "decently and in order" (14:40).

13. How has orderliness in a church service helped you benefit from the service?

The church is called to bring glory to the Lord. One of its foremost duties, then, is worship. This will mean that our church gatherings must essentially be directed upward, to God, not outward, to people. The service should be composed in such a way that He will find the congregation's efforts to be pleasing and in tune with His character.

This is not to imply that there is anything mystical or esoteric about worship, however. First Corinthians 14 distills the necessary elements of worship. The declaration of God's truth is foremost among them. When the saints gather as a church for worship, this is a prime opportunity to "teach others also" (14:19; cf. 2 Tim. 2:2). Then, if "there come in one that believeth not, or one unlearned" (14:24), the people of the congregation will be in a position to share God's saving Word with that person.

If this is the pervading influence in the church, the other components of the service are also sure to edify (cf. 14:26).

The gifts of tongues and prophecy ended when the New Testament was completed. Today, preachers declare God's Word as His fully authoritative message. In doing so, they exercise their spiritual gifts and pray that the lost will trust in the Savior and that the saved will grow spiritually. However, every Christian ought to communicate God's Word by witnessing to the unsaved and encouraging fellow believers.

Yes, every believer has the responsibility to edify other believers. When a church as a whole has this goal, the setting will be conducive to the profitable use of everyone's spiritual gifts.

Making It Personal

14. What are your goals when you attend church?

15. What selfish or sinful goals, if any, do you need to forsake?

16. What opportunities do you have to edify your fellow believers?

17. What opportunities to edify your fellow believers will you take advantage of in the coming week?

18. Memorize 1 Corinthians 14:12.

Up from the Grave

Christ's resurrection guarantees believers a glorious resurrection and provides a reason to serve God together wholeheartedly.

1 Corinthians 15

"But now is Christ risen from the dead, and become the firstfruits of them that slept" (1 Corinthians 15:20).

Jesus Christ rose physically, visibly from death and the grave. This is not a myth or even a historical possibility, but the very basis of our hope as believers and one of the fundamental truths on which the Christian faith stands.

Before Paul closes this magnificent book, he devotes a lengthy chapter to the doctrine of the resurrection. This is a passage and a topic that we often reserve for the Easter season. But this chapter is among the most important in all of sacred Scripture.

Getting Started

1. How important to you is the resurrection of Christ?

2. What difference has the resurrection of Christ made in your life?

Searching the Scriptures

Paul had learned that some in the church at Corinth denied the resurrection of the dead, although they believed in Christ's resurrection (15:12). Since the resurrection of the dead is guaranteed by Christ's resurrection, Paul wrote at length about its reality and its impact on Christian living.

Christ's Resurrection Is Scriptural

The gospel Paul had preached to the Corinthians was pregnant with saving power (15:1, 2), and it was Scriptural. Paul defines it here in these momentous verses. It announced that "Christ died for our sins according to the scriptures; And that he was buried, and that he rose again the third day according to the scriptures" (15:3, 4).

In other words, Christ rose from the dead physically, not merely spiritually, and within history, not as mythology. All the events surrounding His crucifixion and resurrection were completely grounded in Scripture.

3. Read Genesis 3:15; Psalm 22; Isaiah 53; and Mark 15:25–37. How substantiated is the death of Christ in Scripture?

4. Read Psalm 16:10 and John 20:1–19. How substantiated is the resurrection of Christ in Scripture?

5. Read Romans 4:25. What doctrine did Paul link to the resurrection of Jesus Christ?

6. How important is the doctrine of justification?

Christ's Resurrection Is Substantiated

In defense of the resurrection, Paul summoned a host of eyewitness-es to the witness stand. Cephas (Peter) saw the risen Christ. Then all the Twelve saw Him (15:5). Later, more than 500 believers saw Him. Then He was seen by James, Jesus' half-brother. Next, Paul mentioned the entire group of the apostles again as having seen the risen Christ (15:7). Finally, Paul recounted that he saw the risen Christ (15:8). This personal reference recalls Paul's Damascus Road experience (Acts 9:1–9).

7. Why are eyewitnesses crucial in deciding a court case?

8. How important are these witnesses of the resurrection?

How may we have confidence in the reality of Christ's resurrection and base our hope of eternal life upon it? The answer is that we ultimately do so by faith in response to the work of the Holy Spirit, Who uses the Word of God (cf. Rom. 10:17). We must trust in the work of Christ as our only hope of salvation. This is possible through God's gracious work in calling us to Himself (cf. 1 Cor. 1:24); it is not merely the natural outcome of being convinced of the historical fact of the resurrection (cf. 1 Cor. 2:14).

In this manner, the saving grace of the risen Son of God had trans-formed the author of this chapter, Paul, from a lost, spiritually-blind Pharisee to a found and forgiven person in possession of new life and a new ambition. Thus, from the time of his conversion and call to preach the gospel, Paul humbly and devotedly proclaimed the good news about Christ's death, burial, and resurrection (15:9–11).

No one can remove the doctrine of the resurrection from the Bible without also removing hope from the human heart. Apart from the resur-rection, there is no hope of living eternally in Heaven.

The Emptiness of an Occupied Tomb

The resurrection of Christ makes the believer's resurrection possible (cf. John 14:19). More than that, in God's plan, it makes the believer's resurrection an absolute certainty (15:12). Conversely, Paul argues that if we cannot look forward to our resurrection, we must logically look backward to a tomb that still contains the body of the crucified Christ (15:13).

Here again, the Corinthians showed signs of the lingering influence of Greek philosophy, which degraded the body. Apparently, some did not understand that the body will be necessary to fully enjoy a glorified existence in Heaven.

Paul took the occasion of the Corinthians' confusion about the nature of the resurrection body to write this lengthy doctrinal treatise. It constitutes the major passage in the New Testament on the topic of the resurrection. The treatise not only supplies us with much information, but also brings immeasurable comfort to believers.

Paul reveals that a dead Christ would force us to regard our preaching as simply a vain exercise and our faith as a groundless superstition (15:14). Furthermore, a tomb occupied by Christ's dead body declares every Christian witness a liar and pronounces every Christian lost in sin (15:15–17). To make matters worse, if Christ did not overcome death then all our departed Christian friends and family members have entered a doomed eternity (15:18). The lives of Christian servants would be less than meaningless if Christ's body were still lying in the tomb (15:19).

9. What thoughts would go through your mind if you learned the resurrection of Christ was just a hoax?

10. Take a moment to praise God for the confidence you have in the resurrection!

The Fullness of an Unoccupied Tomb

11. Read 1 Corinthians 15:20–23. How does this passage link Christ's resurrection to the resurrection of believers?

Christ's resurrection may be considered the "firstfruits" in at least three ways: 1) His resurrection was the first of its kind—being raised in glorification never to die again (cf. Acts 26:23); 2) His resurrection was the first in priority and position (Col. 1:18); 3) His resurrection was the first of more to come (John 14:19; 1 Cor. 15:23).

Paul assured the Corinthians that Christ is risen from the dead. There is a valid gospel to proclaim, for Christ truly rose, and we can aspire to rise as well. There is hope of life beyond the grave, the prospect of reunion with departed Christian loved ones, and a reason to endure persecution. Drawing from Leviticus 23:10, Paul exclaimed that Christ has "become the firstfruits of them that slept" (1 Cor. 15:20). As death came to all by Adam, so life came to all who are in Christ (15:21).

Notice here that Paul assumes and builds upon the historicity of Adam as the first man and the one, along with Eve, who first sinned. If this is not the case, as some who deny the literal truth of the creation account in Genesis teach, the passage in which Paul is tightly framing his arguments according to history and logic would be meaningless.

The end result of the work of Christ will be to restore mankind to the state he enjoyed before the fall (cf. Matt. 19:28). This is the original perfection of Genesis 1 and 2—a world without sin. Those who deny the literal account of creation in Genesis and teach that there were countless years of death and destruction before the appearance of man and woman would thus also steal our hope of a glorious future in Christ.

12. Read 1 Peter 1:3. What has the resurrection of Christ produced in believers?

13. How is this demonstrated in daily living?

The order of the resurrection and other future events appears in verses 23–28. Paul includes the hope of resurrection for Christians "at his coming" (15:23), as well as the resurrection and judgment of unbelievers that will occur following the millennium (15:25, 26; cf. Rev. 20:5, 6).

The culmination of these future events is the rule of God the Father over all in the eternal kingdom, which will exceed even the glory of the millennial kingdom (1 Cor. 15:24, 27, 28). The resurrection of Christ makes the future, eternal, glorious reign of God possible in this manner.

Christ's resurrection also made baptism meaningful. Paul viewed the ranks of Christians as soldiers engaged in spiritual warfare. As some Christian soldiers died, others stepped in. In baptism, these new believers confessed their faith in the risen Christ and their allegiance to Him (15:29).

14. Read 1 Corinthians 15:31–33. What was Paul willing to do because he knew Christ was raised?

15. When have you witnessed someone with the same sacrificial, bold assurance of Christ's resurrection?

Furthermore, the resurrection of Christ made Paul's perilous life worthwhile. He faced death daily for the sake of the gospel, having turned his back on the allurements of a soft and comfortable life (15:30–32). His reference to fighting wild beasts at Ephesus may be to the wild public demonstration that opposed him when he preached there (Acts 19:23–20:1). Sometimes human foes of the gospel can act like vicious animals.

In verses 33 and 34, Paul called upon the Corinthian believers to turn away from false teachers who denied the resurrection. What they believed about the resurrection would determine how they lived. False teaching would produce false and ungodly living.

Anticipating questions about the resurrection, Paul provided helpful answers. "How are the dead raised up?" was the first question Paul addressed (15:35). He drew upon a principle of nature in doing so. He explained that death always precedes life when a seed is sown (15:36, 37).

Next, Paul answered the anticipated question about what the resurrected body will be like. He explained that there are different kinds of flesh: human flesh, animal flesh, fish flesh, and bird flesh (15:39). Then he pointed out the astronomical and earthly kinds of bodies in the universe. He noted each has a distinct glory (15:40, 41).

Since God has created such a glorious diversity in the universe, He can be trusted to provide glorious resurrection bodies for His people. At the resurrection, a believer's dead body will come out of the grave in a glorified state. It will no longer experience the corruption it underwent in the grave; it will be incorruptible forever (15:42, 43). It will be "a spiritual body" that is fit for use in eternity (15:44).

Drawing from Biblical history, Paul told the Corinthians that Adam became the head of the natural human race. Since the fall, his sinful tendencies and wicked appetites characterize his descendants. Adam's sin became our sin. Then came "the last Adam" (15:45), Christ. All who trust in Christ become a new spiritual race under Christ's headship. The natural preceded the spiritual for all of us believers.

So in the resurrection the change is from the lower, natural order to the higher, spiritual order. Now each of us has a natural body, but in the resurrection each of us will have a spiritual body like Christ has had since His resurrection (15:45–49; cf. Luke 24:13–43; John 20:14–20). Though glorified, each of us will be the exact same person that he or she is now.

16. What aspects of a glorified body are you looking forward to enjoying the most?

When will Christians receive new, glorified, spiritual bodies and "inherit the kingdom of God" (15:50)? Paul associated the time with the Rapture. He presented this truth as a new disclosure, "a mystery" (15:51a). Christians alive on the earth when Christ returns to rapture the church will not experience death but will undergo a dramatic transformation (15:51b).

Instantaneously at Christ's command, the bodies of dead Christians will arise and become incapable of decaying ever again and the bodies of living Christians will be changed to become incapable of dying (15:52, 53; cf. 1 Thess. 4:13–18).

Because the resurrection of Christ assures our resurrection, we need not fear death. When we are resurrected, we will leave death behind as our last unsuccessful foe (15:54). From our perspective, death is like a defanged snake and the grave resembles a prison with its doors removed (15:55). Christ removed the sting of death by dying for us and by rising again. He removed sin's sentence from us and fulfilled the law's demand on our behalf (15:56). Our response is one of thanks to the Lord Jesus Christ for procuring the victory over sin and death for us (15:57).

A Rewarding Ministry

As usual in Scripture, a discussion of the Rapture leads to an appeal for active Christian service. In concluding his teaching about the resurrection, Paul encouraged his readers to maintain a steadfast perseverance.

The Corinthian believers needed to function as a team that was headed for ultimate victory. It was time they put aside their petty differences and joined together in faithful Christian service. They had a big job ahead of them. According to verse 58, the job required being "stedfast" (having a fixed goal), "unmoveable" (unswerving from the faith), and "always abounding in the work of the Lord" (remaining diligent in ministry).

17. What are some good reasons for working for the Lord in the manner described in verse 58?

18. What deters us from working this way as a team of local church believers?

Paul assured the Corinthians their "labour is not in vain in the Lord" (15:58b). Neither is ours. He will honor dedicated Christian teamwork now by helping us fulfill His will. By His power, we will make an impact on our community and even upon the world.

19. If you knew that it would only be a short time until Christ would return, how would you live differently?

Making It Personal

20. What aspects of your daily living reflect your union with the risen Christ?

21. What areas need your attention? Ask Christ to empower you for service and daily living by the Spirit and through the Word.

22. Do you sometimes feel ready to quit serving the Lord? Explain. Let the fact that Christ is alive rekindle your zeal (1 Cor. 15:58).

23. Memorize 1 Corinthians 15:20.

A Heart for Giving

Every Christian should give faithfully to the Lord's work.

1 Corinthians 16

"Upon the first day of the week let every one of you lay by him in store, as God hath prospered him, that there be no gatherings when I come" (1 Corinthians 16:2).

Automatic deposits and automatic bill payment are now an expected convenience. The days of sitting down to write checks for every bill are quickly fading. So should the church adopt the practice of automatically withdrawing church members' offerings from their bank accounts? Would such a practice rob believers of an important opportunity to worship God?

Getting Started

1. What do you think about as the offering plate goes through your row? Do you view the offering as a time of worship?

2. How do you decide how much to put in the offering plate?

Paul addresses giving in the last chapter of his letter to the Corinthians. His brief instructions help us to consider our own giving practices.

Searching the Scriptures

Paul believed the doctrine of the resurrection had practical implications for Christian living. Because Christ arose, we ought to serve Him fervently and faithfully (1 Cor. 15:58), and we ought to consider all of life as a stewardship.

We are stewards of all the resources that God allows us to manage. Unfortunately, some Christians bristle when the topic of giving is introduced, but it ought to be a welcome subject and a happy privilege in view of all that God has given to us.

Give Regularly

The Christians in Jerusalem had fallen upon hard times. They were poverty-stricken and persecuted. So Paul launched a fund drive for them. He wrote to the Corinthian church: "Now concerning the collection for the saints, as I have given order to the churches of Galatia, even so do ye" (16:1).

The collection was to be built by offerings given "upon the first day of the week" (16:2). By following this procedure, the Corinthian Christians would avoid the necessity of taking a last-minute offering when Paul arrived (16:2b). This disciplined pattern of giving shows us how to give. We ought to give regularly to support the Lord's work.

3. What might have been Paul's reason for not wanting the church to collect funds during his visit?

Give Personally

No Christian is exempt from the privilege and responsibility of giving to the Lord's work. Paul told the Corinthian church, "Let every one of you lay by him in store" (16:2).

If anyone considers himself too poor to give, he should consider the condition of the poor widow who dropped all she had into the temple treasury. Jesus did not say she was too poor to give, but rather commended her. He explained that "she of her want did cast in all that she had, even all her living" (Mark 12:44).

4. Since God does not need anything, why does He ask His people to give?

Give Proportionately

The Lord is more concerned about our motive for giving than the amount of our gifts. Second Corinthians 9:7 indicates that we should give "not grudgingly, or of necessity: for God loveth a cheerful giver." Giving reveals our gratitude to the Lord for His blessings (2 Cor. 8:7), and it measures our love (16:24).

Paul did not mention the tithe in 1 Corinthians 16. He instructed that a Christian's guideline for giving should be "as God hath prospered him" (16:2). Giving, then, should be proportionate, but surely one would do well to meet or exceed the basic ten percent required under the Old Testament law (Lev. 27:30). That requirement was also practiced before the law (Gen. 14:18–20) and commended by Jesus (Matt. 23:23).

5. What might be some reasons that people do not give proportionately?

Give Responsibly

Paul's audience in Corinth knew why they were asked to give, where the money was going, and who would carry it to its destination. There was a legitimate need for the money. It was designated for the impoverished Christians in Jerusalem. And men approved by the Corinthian congregation would take it to Jerusalem, possibly accompanied by Paul (16:4). From start to finish, the highest integrity undergirded the project.

At this early date in church history, Paul set high standards for how church funds should be collected, handled, distributed, and accounted for. We can imagine how careful he would have been to make sure that such a situation would not become an opportunity for his apostolic ministry to be disgraced.

A church ought to be wise in its practice of collecting and disbursing the freewill offerings of the Lord's people. The members ought to adopt a budget, share the responsibility of meeting it, and select responsible and highly respected individuals to handle the offerings. Meticulous records, kept up-to-date by financial officers and reported accurately and regularly to the church, will safeguard not only the money but the reputations of those who handle it.

6. What might be some practical applications of Paul's counsel in this section?

There are many excellent resources accessible today for both individuals and churches that need help with any aspect of handling money or becoming better stewards of it. Those who are struggling in this area should seek assistance from some of the widely-regarded ministries and resources that are available to help.

7. Why should a church consider who they could turn to for help with financial issues?

Stewardship of Opportunities

According to 1 Corinthians 16:5–7a, Paul hoped to visit Corinth and spend the winter there. He submitted the matter to the Lord's will. "If the Lord permit," he wrote (16:7b). Until Pentecost, however, he planned to stay at Ephesus (16:8). He recognized the Lord had given him a wide open door of ministry at Ephesus, where he was when he wrote this letter, and he wanted to act as a wise steward of the opportunity (16:9a).

8. What opportunities for service are available in your church and in your community?

Paul understood that opportunity is one of the great spiritual treasures that God gives us. Every true opportunity offers the possibility to accomplish something of eternal value, so Paul approached every opened door as a portico to a new adventure with the Lord (cf. 2 Cor. 2:12; Col. 4:3).

Paul also knew that in God's economy every opportunity is part of the stewardship for which we "shall give account to...God" (Rom. 14:12). With a vision of the awaiting Judgment Seat of Christ clear in his mind, Paul did not want to miss, lose, or waste even one opportunity (9:24–27).

Like Paul, every Christian receives opportunities to minister for the Lord. An opportunity may be as close as next door, where a spiritually hungry neighbor resides. It may be a Sunday School classroom, where a teaching ministry is available. It may be an opportunity to show kindness or an opportunity for personal spiritual growth. Opportunity may even take the form of a new job or an occasion to obtain additional education. A wise Christian must seize the opportunity and rely upon God to accomplish His will in it.

Churches definitely receive opportunities for ministry (cf. Rev. 3:8). They come in many various forms, such as visitors, the sick and suffering in the community, an opening to conduct rescue mission services or chapel services and visitation times at homes for the aging. The weekly worship services and related activities in the church, as well as the ongoing financial support of missionaries, offer tremendous opportunities, if we will simply see them and take hold. A church can seize such opportunities or squander them, but good stewardship always leads a church to do the will of God in ministering to believers and reaching out with the love of Christ to the lost.

9. How does a believer know that an opportunity is given by God?

There is a harsh reality to the issue of opportunity, however. When an opportunity is lost, it may be gone forever. Christ reinforced the urgency of opportunity repeatedly to the seven churches in the book of Revelation. Several decades after Paul wrote 1 Corinthians from Ephesus and contemplated his further ministry there, the risen Christ told the Ephesian church: "Repent, and do the first works; or else I will come unto thee quickly, and will remove thy candlestick out of his place, except thou repent" (Rev. 2:5).

Occasionally, even a good sports team loses a game because of failed opportunities. It is nothing short of tragic if a church squanders its opportunities to serve the Lord successfully.

10. What keeps you from taking advantage of spiritual opportunities?

11. What does it take for a church to be a winning team, capitalizing on every opportunity the Lord gives?

12. How could your church take better advantage of current technologies for the sake of spiritual opportunity?

Paul knew well that the Devil opposes us when we seize opportunities for serving the Lord (cf. 1 Pet. 5:8, 9). He told the Corinthians, "A great door and effectual is opened unto me, and there are many adversaries" (16:9).

As every spiritual leader can attest, there is constant opposition to any attempt at making progress in Christian life and ministry. There will always be enemies of the gospel, there will always be naysayers, there will always be hindrances and there will always be obstacles. These must never be used as excuses for failing to attempt some spiritual accomplishment or there will never be any accomplishment at all (cf. Prov. 22:13; 26:13).

13. What are some of the ways the enemy can oppose a church in its opportunities for service?

Stewardship of Testimony

Paul did not do all the work of the Lord alone; other faithful believers also helped him. Together, Paul and his coworkers were a team. And just as a knowledgeable, humble team leader praises the performance of his teammates, so Paul praised his coworkers.

14. What can we learn from Paul's appreciation for his coworkers?

It seems noteworthy that Apollos, whose following in the church was still significant (cf. 1:12), decided not to go to Corinth in spite of Paul's counsel to him.

Both Timothy and Apollos, however, were strong role models that could help the leaders of the congregation understand how to live out the important commands in 16:13, 14.

Finally, Paul was thankful for Stephanas (1:16), Fortunatus and Achaicus coming to Ephesus to help him (16:15–18).

Paul was joined by a host of believers in greeting the Corinthian church. He wrote, "The churches of Asia salute you." Then he named Aquila and Priscilla, a husband-and-wife team of Christian servants who had opened their home in Ephesus as a place where Christians worshiped and fellowshipped (16:19). This godly couple, originally from Rome, had left Rome when Emperor Claudius ordered the expulsion of Jews from the city. Next, they settled in Corinth, where Paul first met them and resided with them (Acts 18:2). Later, they moved to Ephesus, where they joined Paul here in conveying their goodwill back to Corinth. Finally, after the death of Claudius, they moved back to Rome (Rom. 16:3).

This couple maintained an outstanding testimony wherever they lived. Their example ought to inspire Christian couples today to devote their hearts and homes to the Lord.

All the Christians at Ephesus sent greetings to the church at Corinth (1 Cor. 16:20a). The bonds of Christian love spanned the many miles between the two communities and underscored the truth that Christians are one in Christ.

"Greet ye one another with an holy kiss," Paul told the Corinthians (16:20b). Today, a handshake is the cultural equivalent to the Corinthians' "holy kiss," which merely signified friendship. The Corinthians had alienated and avoided one another. They had quarreled over leadership and practices. It was time for them to show appropriate affection to one another. It is often the case, though, that a church is on shaky ground when its members refuse to shake hands with one another.

The matters contained in the Corinthian letter were so important that Paul signed his name to it (16:21). No one could dispute the letter's authority when they saw his name affixed to it.

Finally, Paul closed the letter with a warning and a benediction.

The Christians were to consider as "Anathema" (16:22), or "accursed," any person who would "love not the Lord Jesus Christ."

"Maranatha," Paul added, meaning, "The Lord is coming," or "Come, Lord" (cf. Rev. 22:20). Paul was anticipating the Lord's return for believers and His judgment on the enemies of the gospel at His coming.

"Maranatha" is a word of hope that reminds us to be ready to meet the Lord at all times. If we do not know where to start preparing for the day of His return, the book of 1 Corinthians certainly gives us much material to consider.

15. Following this study of 1 Corinthians, what areas do you need to work on spiritually in light of the fact that the Lord may return soon?

The epistle closes on a bright, positive note. The Corinthians needed help from their merciful Lord to work through their problems. So

Paul prayed: "The grace of our Lord Jesus Christ be with you" (16:23). Also, the Corinthians needed to know that Paul loved them in spite of the serious tone of his letter, so he wrote as his final words in 1 Corinthians, "My love be with you all in Christ Jesus. Amen" (16:24).

May God help us to continually study and learn from this all-important epistle and then implement its truths in our lives until Christ returns.

Making It Personal

16. If everyone in your church followed your pattern for giving, how would your church do financially?

17. What adjustments do you need to make to your attitude toward giving financially?

18. What adjustments do you need to make to your practice of giving?

19. How often do you think about the ministry opportunities God is bringing your way?

20. What opportunities do you have before you now that you will take advantage of?

21. Memorize 1 Corinthians 16:2.